About the author

Irene Harrell keeps busy as the mother of six children and the wife of a judge who enjoys gardening. When she's not cooking, canning, freezing, or cleaning, she's writing. *God Ventures,* she says, grew out of her awareness of the urgent need for exciting, true, God-with-us-here-and-now material that would hold the attention and capture the hearts of teenagers in her church and community. To do this, she selected stories from such writers as

- Catherine Marshall
- David Wilkerson
- John Sherrill
- Agnes Sanford

as well as lesser known writers whose stories are equally as gripping.

Irene Harrell's two previous books are
Prayerables
Good Marriages Grow
both published by WORD Books.

GOD VENTURES

GOD VENTURES

True Accounts of God in the Lives of Men

Compiled by
Irene Burk Harrell

WORD BOOKS, Publishers
Waco, Texas · London, England

GOD VENTURES

First Printing—May 1970
Second Printing—October 1970

Printed in the United States of America
Library of Congress Catalog Card Number: 76–119888

"A Gentleman in Prison" by Tokichi Ishii is condensed in his own words from his *A Gentleman in Prison,* translated by Caroline Macdonald, published 1922 by (George H. Doran) Harper & Row, New York.

Grateful acknowledgment is made to the following who have granted permission to include the copyrighted selections in this book:

CHRISTIAN LIFE PUBLICATIONS, *Christian Life* Magazine, for "Blizzard," by Ona Lacy Hunter, November 1964; "Four-Footed Angel," by Olive Broadway as told to Esther L. Vogt, November 1965; and "My Grave Was Number 12," by Jonathan Lee as told to Ed Erny, August 1964. Copyright November 1964, November 1965, August 1964 by Christian Life Publications, Inc., Gunderson Drive and Schmale Road, Wheaton, Illinois 60187. Reprinted by permission.

E. P. DUTTON & CO., INC. for "We Thought We Heard the Angels Sing," by Lieutenant James C. Whittaker, condensed in his own words from his *We Thought We Heard the Angels Sing; The Complete Epic Story of the Ordeal and Rescue of Those Who Were With Eddie Rickenbacker on the Plane Lost in the Pacific,* copyright, 1943, E. P. Dutton & Co., Inc. Reprinted by permission of the publishers.

BERNARD GEIS, ASSOCIATES for "Gang War,"* by The Reverend David Wilkerson, taken from *The Cross and the Switchblade* by The Reverend David Wilkerson with John and Elizabeth Sherrill (pp. 86–95), copyright, © 1963 by David Wilkerson. Reprinted by permission of Bernard Geis, Associates.

GUIDEPOSTS for "Race to Save a Traitor," by Dr. Ejnar Lundby as told to Hakan Cronsioe, October, 1966; and "Return from Tomorrow," by George C. Ritchie, Jr., M.D., January, 1966. Copyright, 1966, Guideposts Associates, Inc., Carmel, New York. Reprinted by permission.

Continued on page 6 . . .

To our children

Tommy
Alice
Dino
Susan
'Guerite
Maria

Hodder & Stoughton for "The Ice-Pan Adventure," by Sir Wilfred Grenfell, Chapter XIV of his *The Story of A Labrador Doctor* (pp. 110–117). Copyright, 1925, Hodder & Stoughton, London. Used by permission.

Light & Life Press for "Something Made Me Go," by Mary Aussant. Reprinted by permission from Light & Life Press, Winona Lake, Indiana 46590.

J. B. Lippincott Company for "Birth on Death Row,"* by Agnes Sanford, from her *The Healing Gifts of the Spirit* (pp. 102–105), copyright, © 1966, by Agnes Sanford. Reprinted by permission of J. B. Lippincott Company.

McGraw-Hill Book Company for "Fire"* and "Out of the Dungeon,"* by Catherine Marshall from her *Beyond Ourselves* (pp. 137–39; 242–45), copyright, © 1961, by Catherine Marshall. Used with permission of McGraw-Hill Book Company.
Also for "Cannibal Talk,"* by John L. Sherrill, from his *They Speak in Other Tongues* (pp. 97–100), copyright, © 1964, by John L. Sherrill. Used with permission of McGraw-Hill Book Company.

Moody Press for "Facing Death on the Atlantic," by Dwight L. Moody, from *The Shorter Life of D. L. Moody*, by Arthur Percy Fitts (pp. 100–03). Used by permission, Moody Press, Moody Bible Institute of Chicago.

Simon & Schuster, Inc. for "Christmas Eve Miracle," by Alexander Lake, from his *Your Prayers Are Always Answered* (pp. 69–73), copyright, © 1956, by Alexander Lake. Reprinted by permission of Simon and Schuster, Inc.

These Times for "Am I My Brother's Keeper?" by Cecil Coffey, May, 1966 (pp. 22–23). Used by permission.

* Titles of starred episodes supplied by the compiler.

Contents

Introduction

"IN THE beginning God created. . . ."

Many Christians believe that, but they also think God stopped His creative work "in the beginning." They do not understand that God is still at work in His world.

To show that He is, I have collected true accounts of God in the lives of contemporary people. Their stories are exciting witness and irrefutable evidence that God is still very much alive to those who seek Him.

These people and the dangers they faced as are varied as the places where they experienced God—an Air Corps Lieutenant, his plane down on a sweltering tropical ocean; a doctor, his dog-sled adrift on treacherous ice; a juvenile delinquent ready for gang war in a New York slum; a businessman knotting sheets and blankets to make a rope for escaping a hotel fire; a missionary captured by African cannibals. Their outward circumstances were poles apart, but the heart of their stories is the same: "God is real in my life."

Here are their witnesses. Our lives must make their own.

IRENE BURK HARRELL

GOD VENTURES

Cannibal Talk

JOHN L. SHERRILL

AN ADVENTURE took place in the heart of Africa in the year 1922.

In that year, the Reverend H. B. Garlock and his wife, of Toms River, New Jersey, volunteered for a dangerous assignment: they were to go to Africa as missionaries to the Pahns, a small tribe in the interior of Liberia. No missionaries had ever before worked with the Pahns. The reason was simple. The Pahns were cannibals.

The Garlocks arrived in Liberia and set up camp with a group of African Christians whose tribal boundary touched that of the Pahns. Almost immediately Mrs. Garlock came down with malaria. Their meager medical chest was soon emptied and still her fever rose. Garlock had a difficult time persuading the natives to take a short route to the coast for more medicine because the way led through Pahn country.

At last, however, Garlock convinced the chief that it was possible to skirt the danger areas, and that if medicine didn't arrive soon, Mrs. Garlock might well die. One morning at dawn a group of men left the compound and headed out, filled with misgivings, to bring back supplies.

About noon the head carrier suddenly appeared in the doorway of the mud hut where Mrs. Garlock lay. He was out of breath. In gasps he blurted out what had happened. One of his men had been captured by the cannibals. The African assured the two missionaries that unless the man could be rescued, he would be eaten.

Garlock realized that it was his fault. Providentially, his wife's fever had begun to go down that very morning, within an hour after the supply party had left. Without hesitation Garlock himself set out into Pahn territory, taking along a few hand-picked warriors: he was going to try to get the man out.

Just before dark, the little group arrived at the village where the carrier was being held. A wooden fence ran around the cluster of huts, but no one stood guard. Garlock peeked cautiously through and saw that one of the huts had sentries posted before it. Two men carrying spears squatted outside in the dust. Their hair was braided in long pigtails; their front teeth were filed to a point.

That would be the prison, Garlock decided. He turned to his men. "I'm going in," he whispered. "If there's trouble make as much noise as you can. I'll try to get away in the confusion."

Garlock was counting on two facts to help him. One was the probability that the Pahns had never seen a white man: he hoped that this would give him the advantage of surprise. The other was that he believed the miracle stories of the Bible, telling of supernatural help coming when it was needed most. Garlock was praying as he stepped into the cannibals' compound. He was praying that God would show him step by step what he should do.

Walking as straight and as tall as he could, he strode directly toward the prison hut. The guards were too astonished to stop him. He walked between them and ducked inside the hut. Outside, he heard the guard begin to shout: he heard feet slap against the packed earth as others ran to join them. In the dark interior Garlock crawled forward until his hands touched a figure tied to the center pole of the hut.

Garlock slipped a knife out of his pocket and cut the bonds. The carrier spoke to him. But he seemed incapable of making any effort in his own behalf. Garlock dragged the terrified man out through the door. But that's as far as he got. There in the courtyard was a yelling, threatening crowd of Africans armed with knives, spears and hatchets.

Garlock listened for his own men to start a distraction. But outside the compound all was silence. Garlock knew that he had been abandoned.

There was nothing for it except to try a bluff. With great deliberation he settled the prisoner up against the hut, and then he himself sat down on the skull of an elephant that stood beside the door. All the while he was praying. The crowd kept its distance, still yelling and milling, but not coming close.

A full moon rose. Garlock sat quietly on his elephant's skull. Finally the people squatted down in a great semicircle facing the hut. In the center of this ring, Garlock thought he spotted the chief and beside him the village witch doctor.

Suddenly this man stood up. He ran a few steps toward Garlock, then stopped. He held out a reed wand, shook it at Garlock, then started to stalk back and forth between the missionary and the chief, talking loudly and gesturing occasionally toward the prisoner. Garlock could not understand a word he said, but it was clear to him that he was on trial.

The witch doctor harangued Garlock for an hour, and then quite abruptly he stopped. He came, for the first time, directly up to Garlock and peered into his face. The witch doctor thrust his neck forward, then drew it back amid the cheers of the onlookers. Then, with great ostentation, he laid the wand on the ground at Garlock's feet. He stepped back, waiting.

Silence fell over the tribe. Garlock gathered that it was now time for him to speak in his own defense.

But how! Garlock did not know one word of the Pahn language. The crowd began to grow restless. Stalling for time Garlock stood up and picked up the wand. Instantly the natives fell silent. And while they waited, Garlock prayed.

"Lord, show me what to do. Send your Spirit to help me."

Suddenly Garlock began to shake violently. This frightened him as he did not want the others to see that he was afraid. But with the trembling came a sense of the nearness of the Holy Spirit. Words of Jesus came to him: "Take no thought what ye shall speak, neither do ye premeditate; but whatsoever shall be given to you in that hour, that speak ye; for it is not ye that speak but the Holy Ghost."

Garlock felt a strange boldness. He took a deep breath and began to speak. From his lips came a flow of words which he did not understand.

Garlock saw the natives lean forward, enthralled. He saw that the words—whatever they were—had a stirring effect on those who listened. He knew beyond a doubt that he was speaking to the Pahns in their own language.

For twenty minutes Garlock talked to the Pahns. Then, as suddenly as the speech-power came, it vanished, and Garlock knew that he had come to the end of his discourse. He sat down.

There was a moment of waiting while the chief and the witch doctor put their heads together. Then, straightening, the witch doctor gave an order and a white rooster was brought forward. With a snap, the witch doctor wrung the rooster's neck. He sprinkled some of the blood on the foreheads of Garlock and the prisoner. Later Garlock interpreted this as meaning that the rooster had taken his place: blood had to be shed, but something he had said while speaking in the Spirit had convinced these people that he and the prisoner should go free.

A few minutes later, Garlock and the captured man were walking through the jungle back toward the mission station. The chief had even supplied two of his own men to guide them the first part of the journey. In time, the Pahns gave up their cannibal life and were converted to Christianity. Garlock is certain that the beginnings of the conversion came with the seed sown while he stood in a flood of moonlight and gave a speech, not one word of which did he understand.

Something Made Me Go

MARY AUSSANT

OH, *that bothersome phone! Why does it always have to ring right at closing time?* Wondering who wanted a payroll check or information about an unpaid voucher, I picked up the receiver.

"Army Finance, Disbursing Section," I said. "Yes, this is Mary." The voice at the other end was unfamiliar, and I couldn't imagine who would be calling for me by my first name. I knew that Tiny and I had a movie date at eight o'clock, but this wasn't Tiny.

"I'm Jim Thornton, a friend of Tiny's—he's been in a wreck." The voice faltered, then went on. "It's bad—real bad. I was at the hospital when they brought him in. He asked me to tell you he won't be able to make it tonight."

He kept talking, making it unnecessary for me to ask any questions. "Tiny was hit by a train at the crossing outside Anchorage this afternoon. His truck is a total loss—the train dragged it down the tracks. The only reason Tiny's alive is because he was thrown out of the truck. Both his arms and legs are broken—his shoulders and knees crushed. He's conscious but on the critical list. We'll know about internal injuries when the doctors get the x-ray reports."

I tried to swallow, but couldn't.

"I don't know any more to tell you, Miss, but—well, would you like for me to take you to the hospital?" The voice waited.

Blood was pounding in my heart, and the telephone receiver shook in my hand. *Tiny? Tiny hurt?* Dear God.

"Oh, yes," I breathed and shut my eyes. I was so thankful to have someone to go with me.

The nurse let us in. "You may stay for just a minute." she said. "To let him know you're here. He's in the fifth bed on the left."

We walked into the critical ward. The first things I saw were two huge, pasty-white feet sticking out from under an olive drab blanket. Then my eyes traveled up the large body, all six feet three inches of it. I wondered who had nicknamed him Tiny!

"Sorry, I couldn't make it tonight, Mary." Tiny's eyes had opened for an instant, then closed again. A shudder ran through his body.

I wanted to speak, but what could I say? I looked at Jim. He was shaking his head. It was bad.

As we turned to go, I managed, "Tiny—we're here. Remember that we're here."

Jim had to lead me out. Tears were blinding me as the cold Alaska night closed around us.

For the next two weeks we visited Tiny, watching him fight for life. Some nights we felt he knew we were there—even though he had lapsed into unconsciousness. Each night I whispered close to his ear, "We're here, Tiny, we're here."

I knew that Tiny was fighting; and if anyone could make it, he could. As I stood by his bed one night, I saw his eyelids flutter open. He looked at me and spoke—his voice was weak, but he spoke. I knew then that Tiny would live—but I didn't know then that I would have a part in it.

Trips to the hospital became more and more hazardous as winter settled down bringing much snow and bitter cold. Jim and I discussed Tiny's slow progress. He would live, but could he ever walk again? His knees had been crushed. Could the doctors perform a miracle? We prayed that they could.

Then came the night when Tiny told us that he was off the critical list and would be transferred to the recovery ward the next day. I was elated.

The next night a bitter storm was raging. Snow had fallen most of the afternoon and the wind was ferocious. The temperature was 'way down. Could I make the trip to the hospital safely by myself? Jim was busy and couldn't go with me.

The wind howling outside tempted me to get into my fleecy bathrobe and warm slippers, but *something* made me pull on my fur-lined boots and reach for my heavy parka and gloves.

An icy blast hit me when I opened the door. I slammed it shut and shivered as I pulled my gloves off again. *No need to go out tonight,* I reasoned. *Tiny's off the critical list. I can see him tomorrow*. But *something* insisted.

"Oh, all right," I muttered, grumbling as I struggled with the car door. Whatever *something* was making me go wouldn't take "no" for an answer.

The road was barely visible as the snow whirled across the countryside. More than once I felt the car slip, but I kept doggedly on and finally reached the hospital. Inside and thawed out, I was eager to see Tiny in his new ward. I hurried down the long hall. A corpsman directed me to Tiny's ward, and I had no trouble in finding it. I heard a deafening blast of music. They were showing a movie.

As I entered the ward, my eyes had to adjust to the darkness. I asked for Tiny and was led to a small cubicle at the end of the ward. Then I saw a young man standing over Tiny, giving him his first good shave in weeks.

But what was wrong with Tiny? His chest heaved—his breath came in agonizing gasps. Hadn't anyone noticed? Why weren't they doing something? I'd have to get help, but I didn't want to alarm Tiny. I faked a smile and patted his hand. "I'll come back after you've had your shave," I lied. Then I ran down the hallway and found the head nurse.

"Something has happened to Sgt. Thomas!" I almost shouted at her. "He can hardly breathe! Get him back to the critical ward! Call the doctor!" I was giving orders, then pleading with her. "He's going to die down there in that noisy ward."

She looked at me as if she thought I'd lost my mind.

"Why," she explained gently, "Tiny was fine just a little while ago. And I don't have the authority to move him—only the chief of the hospital can give that order. He's gone to his quarters for the night, and I wouldn't dare disturb him—except for an emergency."

She looked questioningly at me again and saw that her words hadn't calmed me at all. "This *is* an emergency," I insisted, thinking of Tiny gasping for breath. "Tiny has pneumonia—or something worse."

I could see she was weakening, but I still hadn't convinced her of the urgency of the situation. "I'll take a look at him—later—just as soon as I can," she said, walking in the other direction. "But first I have to check on the other patients in the critical ward." The door closed on her and on hope.

Something told me that later might be too late. Someone had to act, immediately—or Tiny would die! If she couldn't act, I'd have to.

I rushed to the telephone down the hall and lifted the receiver. "Operator—this is an emergency—give me the chief of the hospital at once."

"I'm calling from the hospital," I told the chief. "I've just visited Sgt. Thomas. He's dying. Do something!"

I hung up before he could ask any questions. I knew he couldn't ignore my call. Seconds, that seemed like forever, passed. Then I heard a phone ring. There were hurrying feet and then two white coated men wheeled a stretcher down the hall. Tiny was on it.

I breathed a prayer of thanksgiving and sank down on a bench to wait—and to pray. A half hour passed. I could feel the cold seeping in through the cracks of the floor of the old building. I waited another hour. Surely someone would come soon to let me know what was going on.

Finally the head nurse appeared from around the corner. She looked pale, but smiling as she approached me and took my hands in hers. "You've saved Tiny's life tonight," she said. "He had blood clots in his lungs. They were coming from his badly crushed knees. The doctors are still working to tie off the veins that are taking the clots to his upper body. But it's under control now."

I heaved a mighty sigh of relief, and she said, "Thanks—thanks for all you did. Tiny will want to thank you too when he knows. I'll pay more attention to people than to red tape from now on," she promised.

I nodded unable to do anything more. Later, when I stumbled out the door into the biting cold, I saw the snow had stopped. The stars were little torches flaming in the sky—and then my eye caught flashes of rainbow-colored northern lights streaking out of the north. They danced and played among the stars as I watched. Were they a good omen? A promise, like the rainbow for Noah? Surely they had to be.

Four months later Tiny walked out of the hospital on long wobbly legs—but he walked. After several weeks he came to my office.

"You saved my life," he said shyly, "and I've come to say 'thank you.' I'm being shipped out to Walter Reed Hospital where they can do some final repairs on my old bones." He braced himself on one of his crutches and extended his hand for a final farewell.

I waved goodbye as Tiny limped out the door. My heart was glad, remembering the "something" that would not let me stay at home on that blizzardy night when Tiny almost died. I knew, beyond a doubt, that the "something" was God.

Gang War

THE REVEREND DAVID WILKERSON

IT FELT GOOD to drive over the George Washington Bridge again, and later over the Brooklyn Bridge. It was good to walk through the streets again, jumping over piles of snow as I had done when I first came to the city. I was surprised at how much at home I felt. I wanted to look up old friends. I wanted to revisit sites where miracles had happened in the hearts of boys.

One of these sites was the Fort Greene Projects. I was walking down the street, reliving the scene Jimmy Stahl and I had enacted there, when suddenly I heard my name called.

"Davie! Preacher!"

I turned and saw two fine-looking Negro soldiers approaching me at a run. They were wearing neat, freshly pressed uniforms and their shoes shone till it hurt the eye.

I stared at them. "Buckboard! Stagecoach!" I hardly recognized them: they must have put on twenty pounds each.

"Yessir," they said together, coming to a snappy attention. "Look good, eh Davie?"

Getting into the Army is a kind of ultimate for many boys from the housing projects. The literacy and health requirements are stiff enough so that it is considered a Certificate of Worth to be able to wear a uniform. Buckboard, Stagecoach and I had a great reunion. They told me they were doing real well. They told me they quit the gang after our street meeting and never went back.

"In fact, Preach," said Stagecoach, "the Chaplain gang broke up for the rest of the summer. Nobody felt like fighting."

I left Buckboard and Stagecoach with real regret. I was surprised at the strength of my own reactions to this unexpected meeting. I had liked these boys and missed them more than I had known.

But the great surprise was ahead for me.

I set out down Edward Street, past the lamp post where Jimmy and I had preached, looking for Israel and Nicky. I saw a young Spanish lad I thought I recognized and asked him if he knew the whereabouts of Nicky and Israel of the Mau Maus.

The boy looked at me oddly. "You mean those jitterbuggers who turned saints?" He meant it as a joke but my heart leaped. "Glory to God!" I thought. "They're holding on!"

But the next piece of news left me reeling. Not only were they holding on, but Nicky, at any rate, was going places.

"Nicky, huh!" said the boy with a disdainful snort. "He's crazy. He's going to be one of these nutty preachers."

I stood on the street with my mouth hanging open. "Did I hear you right? Nicky wants to become a *preacher?*"

"That's what he says."

Where could I find him, I wanted to know. When had he talked about preaching? Who had he talked to? Had he taken any first steps? The boy couldn't answer me, so I took off and looked for Nicky myself.

I found him a little later, sitting on some apartment-house steps and talking to another boy.

"Nicky?" I said.

Nicky turned around, and I stared into a face I didn't know.

Where the hard, defensive exterior had been, there was openness and animation, a charming and eager boy's face. Now his eyes lit up with real joy.

"Preacher!" He hopped up and ran toward me. "Davie!" He turned to the boy who was with him. "Look, man! This is the preacher I told you about. This is the one who bugged me."

It was wonderful to see him. After introductions and polite talk, I asked Nicky if it was true that he wanted to go into the ministry.

Nicky looked down at the sidewalk. "I never wanted anything so bad, Davie," he said.

"This is just terrific news!" I said. "Tell me, have you done anything about it yet?"

"I don't know how to start."

I was overflowing with ideas. I offered to write to some theological schools. I wanted to sponsor him myself. I wanted him to go to a voice clinic for his impeded speech. I even had some thoughts about raising the necessary money for all this. I had been invited to speak to a church group in Elmira, New York, a few weeks from then, on the problems of young people in the cities. It struck me as ironic that in that same city, Luis Alvarez had been imprisoned. The boys don't stay long in Elmira. Luis would be transferred by now; I had no idea where he was.

"Nicky," I said, "will you come with me to Elmira? Will you tell your story to the people there? It could be that they'll be able to help you."

I had no sooner made the suggestion than I began to have qualms about it. Nicky's story, as it had come to me in bits and pieces, was an exceedingly ugly one, full of a brutality and a strange irrationality that might be well-nigh incomprehensible in Elmira, New York. I was accustomed by now to chilling sights and sounds on New York's streets, and even I found his story shocking.

Still, I argued with myself, the Elmira church had expressed a desire to learn about the gangs: here indeed would be a speedy introduction. For me it would mean a chance to hear Nicky's story from start to finish as I had not yet done, and best of all, a chance to see the St. Nick experience from the other side.

So that was how Nicky came to be standing on a platform in Elmira, New York, a few weeks later, to relate the story of his life. I had spent some time on his introduction, stressing the poverty and loneliness that spawned boys like this so that the audience would not judge him too harshly before they heard him through.

My precautions were unnecessary. From the moment he began to speak, that roomful of people was with him. His own words, the pathetic narrowness of his experience—for all he was so knowing—the flat, staccato recital by a boy who had not learned to exaggerate or embellish, told more than volumes of sociology about the world he came from.

"I was mostly in the streets," he began, "because my parents had customers coming where we lived. They would come at night or in the day and then all of us kids had to go out. They were spiritualists, my parents. They advertised in the Spanish papers that they would talk with the dead and cure sickness, and they would also give advice about money and family problems.

"There was only one room at home, so us kids were in the street. At first the other kids beat me up and I was afraid all the time. Then I learned how to fight and they were scared of me and they left me alone. After a while I got so I liked it better in the street than I did at home. At home I was the youngest one. I was nothing. But in the street they knew who I was.

"My family moved a lot and mostly it was on account of me. If there was any trouble the police would come around asking questions and then the superintendent wherever we lived would go to my parents and say we had to move. They didn't want their building to have trouble with the police. It was that way if the police just asked a Puerto Rican boy a question. It didn't matter if he did anything, the minute the police came around asking about him, he and his family had to get out.

"I didn't know why I acted like I did. There was a thing inside me that scared me. It worried me all the time but I couldn't stop it. It was this feeling I got if I saw a cripple. It was a feeling like I wanted to kill him. It was that way with blind people, too, or real little kids—anyone weak or hurt—I would hate them.

"One day I told my old man about this thing. We never talked or anything, but this thing scared me. So I told him and he said I had a devil. He tried to call the devil out of me, but it wouldn't come.

"The crazy thing in me got worse and worse. If someone had crutches I would kick them or if an old man had a beard I would try to pull it out and I would rough up little kids. And all the while I would be scared and wanting to cry, but the thing inside me was laughing and laughing. The other thing was blood. The minute I saw blood I would begin to laugh and I couldn't stop it.

"When we moved into the Fort Greene Projects, I went in with the Mau Maus. They wanted me to be President. But in a rumble the President has to direct traffic (give orders) and I wanted to fight. So they made me Vice-President.

"I was also Sergeant-at-Arms. That meant I was in charge of the arsenal. We had garrison belts and bayonets and switch-blades and zip guns. I liked to go in and just look at those things. You steal a car aerial to make the zip guns. You use a door latch for the trip hammer and they shoot .22 shells.

"But for rumbling I liked a baseball bat. I'd cut a hole in a garbage can to see out, then I'd put it over my head and swing the bat. The Mau Maus would never fight alongside me because when I got crazy like that I would beat on anybody.

"I also learned how to stick with a knife which is when you cut someone but don't kill him. I stuck sixteen people, and I was in jail twelve times. Some of those times my picture was in the paper. When I walked down the street everyone knew me and the mothers would call their little kids.

"The gangs knew me too. One day when I was waiting for a subway five guys came up behind me. They got a leather belt around my neck and kept twisting it. I didn't die, but I used to wish I had because after that I could never talk right. There was a funny noise in my throat. I had this hate of people who had anything wrong with them, and now it was me. I had to bop all the time, after that, to keep respect.

"Our gang controlled the turf as far as Coney Island and Ralph Avenue. We had red jackets with MM on them and we wore continental heels, which are good in a fight. One day we were in a candy store on Flatbush Avenue. There were six of us, drinking soda, when seven Bishops walked in. The Bishop gang was at war with the Mau Maus.

"One of the Bishops went up to the candy counter like he owned it. My boys were watching me. I walked over and I shoved him. He shoved back and then everyone was fighting. The owner's wife started screaming. All the other customers ran out on the sidewalk. There was a butcher knife on the counter. One of the boys picked it up and cut a Bishop five times through the scalp. I saw the blood and I started to laugh. I knew he was dead and I was scared but I couldn't stop laughing. The owner's wife was telephoning the police. Another one of my boys picked up that butcher knife and hit her right in the stomach. Then we ran.

"I never touched the knife so I didn't go to jail. But my parents had to go to the court and I guess it was the first time they looked at me. They got scared when they saw what I was. They decided to get out of New York and go back to Puerto Rico. My brother and I went to the airport to say good-bye to them. On the way back from the airport in his car he gave me a .32 pistol. He said, 'You're on your own, Nick.'

"The first thing I had to do was find a place to sleep. I held up a guy with the gun and got ten dollars. I rented a room on Myrtle Avenue. I was sixteen then. That's how I lived after that, holding up guys for money or something to hock.

"During the day it was all right. I was with the gang. Whatever the President and I told them to do they would do. But at night, when I had to go into that room, it was terrible. I would think about the two dead people in the candy store. I would bang my head on the floor to stop thinking about them. I started waking up in the middle of the night, crying for my mother. We never talked, or anything, before she left, but suddenly I felt like she should come and take care of me.

"I turned eighteen in July, 1958. That month the Dragons from the Red Hook projects killed one of our boys. We were going down on the subway to get one of them. That's gang law: if one Mau Mau dies, one Dragon dies. We were walking down Edward Street on our way to the subway station when we saw a police car stopped and a whole bunch of Chaplains hanging around. The Chaplains are the Nigger gang in Fort Greene. We had a treaty with them that we wouldn't fight and we would work together if another gang invaded us.

"It looked like action so we went over. The Chaplains were all standing around two guys I never seen, one had a bugle and the other was a real skinny guy. Then somebody brought an American flag and the police car drove away. All it was, the two guys wanted to hold a street meeting.

"As soon as the flag came the skinny guy got up on a chair, opened up a book, and this is what he read out of it:

For God so loved the world that He gave His only begotten Son, that whosoever believeth in Him should not perish.

" 'Now,' the preacher said, 'I'm going to talk to you about "Whosoever." "Whosoever" means Negroes and Puerto Ricans, and especially it means gang members. Do you know that when they crucified Jesus they crucified gang members, too? One on each side of Him . . .'

"I'd had enough. I said, 'Come on you guys, we got business.'

"Not one of them moved. It was the first time they didn't follow me. Then I got scared and I called that preacher every filthy name I knew. He paid no attention, just kept on talking, a long time.

"And the next thing you knew the President of the Chaplains flopped down on his knees, right on Edward Street, and started crying. The Vice-President and two War Lords got down beside him and they cried. One thing I couldn't stand was crying. I was glad when the Chaplains left. I figured we would go too.

"But then this preacher comes up to Israel—he was President of the Mau Maus—and starts shaking his hand. I figured he was trying to bust us up and I went up and shoved the preacher. Israel stared at me like he'd never seen me before.

"So that preacher heads for me. 'Nicky,' he says, 'I love you.'

"No one in my life ever told me that. I didn't know what to do. 'You come near me, preacher,' I said, 'I'll kill you!' And I meant it. Well, Israel and the preacher talked some more, but at last he left and I thought it was over. Only we never went after the Dragons.

"But later this preacher came back and he talked about this big meeting for gangs they were going to have up in Manhattan, and how we should come. 'We'd like to come, Preach,' says Israel, 'but how we going to get through Chink town?' 'I'll send a bus for you,' says the preacher. So then Israel said we'll come.

"Well, I said, not me. I felt like I'd rather die than go to that meeting. But when the gang went it turned out I was with them. I was scared not to be with the gang. I figured I would fix his little prayer-meeting for him. When we got there here were three rows of seats right down front roped off for us. That surprised me some. The preacher said he'd save us seats but I never figured he'd do it.

"A lady was playing the organ and I got the guys stamping and shouting for action. Then a little girl came out on the stage and began to sing. I whistled at her and everyone laughed. It was all going my way and I was feeling good.

"Finally the preacher came out and he said, 'Before the message tonight we're going to take up a collection.'

"Well I figured I saw his angle. I'd been wondering all along what was in this for him. Now I saw he was a moneygrabber like everyone else.

" 'We're going to ask the gang members themselves to take it up,' he says. 'They'll bring the money around behind this curtain and up onto the stage.'

"I figured he didn't have any good sense: anyone could see there was a door back there!

" 'May I have six volunteers?' he says.

"Man, I was on my feet in a second. I pointed out five of my boys and we piled down there quick. Here was my chance to make him look silly. He gave us cardboard cartons. I wanted to get started right away but he made us stand there while he reeled off a long blessing. I tried not to laugh.

"Well, we worked that whole arena. If I didn't like what someone put in, I just stood there till he gave some more. They all knew Nicky. Then we met down behind the curtain.

"There was the door. It was wide open. I could see streetlights and I heard a water truck spraying the street. Back in the arena some of them were laughing. They knew what we were pulling. My boys were watching me, waiting the word to cut out.

"And I just stood there. I didn't know what it was; I had a funny feeling. Suddenly I knew what it was: that preacher trusted me. That never happened in my life before and I just stood there, my boys watching me.

"Inside, I could hear they were giving him a hard time. They were shouting and stamping and he having to stand there and face them, trusting me.

" 'All right, you guys,' I said. 'We're going up on that stage.'

"They looked at me like I wasn't right in my head, but they

never argued. I was that kind of guy that the kids didn't argue with. We went up the stairs and you never heard a place get quiet so fast. We gave him the cartons. 'Here's your money, Preacher,' I said.

"He just took the money, not surprised or anything, like he knew all the time I'd bring it.

"Well, I went back to my seat and I was thinking harder than I ever thought before. He started talking and it was all about the Holy Spirit. The preacher said the Holy Spirit could get inside people and make them clean. He said it didn't matter what they'd done, the Holy Spirit could make them start new, like babies.

"Suddenly I wanted that so bad I couldn't stand it. It was as if I was seeing myself for the first time. All the filth and the hate and the foulness like pictures in front of my eyes.

" 'You can be different!' he said. 'Your life can be changed!'

"I wanted that; I needed that, but I knew it couldn't happen to me. The preacher told us to come forward if we wanted to be changed but I knew it was no use for me.

"Then Israel told us all to get up. 'I'm President,' he said, 'and this whole gang is going up there!'

"I was the first one at the rail. I kneeled down and said the first prayer of my life and this was it: 'Dear God, I'm the dirtiest sinner in New York. I don't think You want me. If You do want me, You can have me. As bad as I was before, I want to be that good for Jesus.'

"Later the preacher gave me a Bible and then I went home wondering if the Holy Ghost was really inside me, and how I would know. The first thing that happened, when I went in my room and shut the door I didn't feel scared. I felt like I had company in the room—not God or anyone like that, but the way I'd feel if my mother came back. I had four pot sticks (marijuana cigarettes) in my pocket. I ripped them up and threw them out the window.

"The next day everyone was staring because word had gone

around that Nicky had religion. But another thing happened that made me know it was real. Little kids would always run when they saw me, but on that day two little boys stared at me a minute and then they came right up to me. They wanted me to measure and see which one of them was taller—nothing important. Only I put my arms around them because I knew then I was different, even if it didn't show except to kids.

"Then, a few weeks later, a Dragon came up to me and he said, 'Is it true you don't carry weapons any more?' I told him it was true, and he pulled a ten-inch knife and went for my chest. I threw my hand up and caught the knife there. I don't know why, but he ran, and I stood there, looking at the blood coming from my hand. I remembered how blood always made me go crazy, but that day it didn't. Words came into my mind that I had read in my Bible, 'The blood of Jesus Christ cleanseth us from all sin.' I ripped my shirt and tied up my hand and from that day blood never bothered me."

As Nicky talked, a hush fell over the room—the scarcely breathing silence that invariably attends a miracle. For we were witnessing a miracle—or hearing one—that night in Elmira; and as each of the listeners took it in, he caught his breath with the little gasp that sends the knowledge racing through the room.

Nicky's voice, the straining, painful, stammering voice in which he had begun his story, had altered as he spoke. Gradually the words came more readily, the sounds clearer, until he was speaking as distinctly and effortlessly as anyone in the room. Only now had Nicky himself realized it. He stood on the platform trembling, unable to go on, tears streaming down his face.

I never knew what had caused his speech problem, whether it was physical injury resulting from the strangling, or what doctors term an "hysterical" affliction. Nicky, of course, never in his wildest fancies considered seeing a doctor about it. I only know that, from that night on, his voice was healed.

That night, too, a collection was taken in Elmira which started Nicky on a long and remarkable journey.

Race to Save a Traitor

DR. EJNAR LUNDBY as told to HAKAN CRONSIOE

WHEN I SAW the gray walls of the prison ahead, I wanted to turn my car around and forget the assignment. How could I marshall any compassion for a traitor and murderer?

Yet the call had come from Bishop Eyvind Berggrav himself. "Doctor Lundby," he had said, "a man by the name of Kristian Hilmer is to be executed in a few days at Grini. Will you go and see him?"

The Bishop had often asked me to give spiritual counsel to men in this prison just outside of Oslo. But during the final days of World War II Kristian had taken part in the bombing of a building used by Norwegian patriots. One man had been killed. He had done heroic work in the Norwegian underground during the war, and I had admired him greatly. To minister to his assassin seemed beyond my power. Yet I had to go.

When I was ushered into Kristian's cell, the prisoner was lying on his bed staring at the ceiling.

"Kristian, is there any way I can help you?"

The answer was a curse.

I stood there silently for a moment, then suddenly realized

that my personal emotions were in God's way. I prayed for compassion on my part—and it came. Then I prayed for Kristian's soul.

I had brought a Bible which I laid on the table.

"Kristian, you may not want to listen to my words. That's all right. I am only a human. But I've brought you the words of One who is divine and who can help you because He cares for you in spite of all you have done."

At this Kristian sat up on his bed and stared morosely at me. Then he looked at the Bible, and I had a feeling he was going to throw it at me. But suddenly he shrugged and lay down again.

I left.

The next day a friend invited me to go with him to Switzerland for a conference. He had bought tickets, and I was about to accept when something stopped me. To my astonishment I felt the strongest kind of inner guidance that I should go and see Kristian again.

Perhaps I should explain a little of my belief in guidance. Until 1934 I had been an unbeliever. Then some people of the Oxford Group* had come to Oslo to hold meetings. A friend persuaded me to attend one night which I did halfheartedly. The sincerity and honesty of these people penetrated my defenses. I soon became a Christian—an enthusiastic Christian.

One of the cardinal tenets of the Oxford Group was that God can and does give guidance to individuals. I was skeptical of all this at first because I felt that human desires could so easily be interpreted as God's guidance. But as I saturated myself with Scripture and developed prayer periods of quiet listening for an inner voice, I began to receive nudgings and communications which I could not explain in terms of my scientific training.

But the real test of these "communications" came when I began to act on them, timidly at first, then boldly. During the

* A world-wide movement, started at Oxford University in the 1920's, to deepen the spiritual lives of nominal Christians.

following years I was used by God in some remarkable ways to lead other people into Christianity.

Therefore, when I felt an inner insistence that I go to see Kristian again, I decided to obey. My friend went on to Switzerland without me.

When I appeared at the prison the next day, the change in Kristian startled me. Something had happened to him overnight. He was washed, shaved, and his hair was combed. "Hello, Doctor Lundby," he said warmly.

He expressed gratitude for the Bible which he had been reading. Quietly we talked together. To my surprise he was hungry to know about Jesus Christ and right there accepted Him as Lord. We prayed together, and as we parted Kristian said, "I am ready now to die for the crime I committed."

A few minutes later, as I was leaving through the prison yard, I stopped suddenly. "Kristian lied to you," said a voice inside me.

I was confused and annoyed. I didn't want to accept this guidance from God at all. "He has just become a Christian. Why would he lie?" I found myself answering.

But the inner voice was persistent. "He lied . . . he lied."

Reluctantly I returned to Kristian's cell. He was staring at the open Bible. "Kristian, did you lie to me a few minutes ago?" I asked.

Startled, he looked up at me, then back again at his Bible. "How incredible that my lie should be exposed twice at the same time," he said.

Then he read these verses from the 42nd chapter of Job: *Who is he that hideth counsel without knowledge? Therefore have I uttered that I understood not.*

Pale and shaken, Kristian explained that his acceptance of Christ had been sincere. But he had lied about the bombing. He had been forced only to drive the car. The actual killer had escaped.

"Why didn't you tell the truth at the trial?" I asked.

Kristian explained that the bomber had a family to care for. "I am single."

I wasn't satisfied with this explanation, wondering if there was pressure on him to remain silent. But I was convinced that an innocent man was about to die for a crime he did not commit—unless I could do something.

At first Kristian did not want to tell me the name of the real killer. Awed by God's intervention, however, he finally gave it to me—Henrik Bakke, who lived 200 miles to the north.

Then Kristian reached for my hand. "Up to now I've never cared much whether I lived or died," he said. "But you have helped me find a reason to live. Is there any hope?"

"There is always hope," I said. But to myself I questioned: what could I do in two days?

There was no question as to my next step. Kristian's execution was three days off. I got in my car and headed north.

It took most of a day to discover that Henrik Bakke was in the local hospital. Only because I was a doctor did I gain entrance to his room. One look at Henrik lying in bed and my heart sank. He was a very sick man. I spoke to him quietly.

"Mr. Bakke, are you going to let Kristian Hilmer die for a crime you committed?"

The figure on the bed stirred. Two dull eyes stared up at me. The lips moved. "Who told you?" he asked hoarsely.

"Kristian did. He will die in two days unless you confess."

The figure in bed shrugged. "I'll be dead then, too, probably."

My hands were sweating with tension. "Don't you want to do one good thing before you die?"

Bakke stared at me for a long moment. "What?"

"Sign a confession."

"All right."

I reached for some paper, but he shook his head. "Not now. Tomorrow."

"Tomorrow may be too late."

His eyes were losing interest. "Tomorrow or not at all."

I looked at him in frustration but knew there was nothing more I could do then.

That night, I wrote out a confession for Bakke to sign and arrived at the hospital at daybreak. The nurse at the desk shook her head. "Sorry, Doctor Lundby. Mr. Bakke passed away during the night."

I returned to Oslo and in desperation called the President of the High Court. He was sympathetic but said nothing could be done without new evidence. Depressed, I went to my room to pray and meditate. Kristian's execution was set for noon the following day.

That night I was scheduled to give a talk in a downtown church. I reached for the phone to cancel out, but was stopped by the inner voice.

For some reason God wanted me to go. Over and over I have battled with the human me when God is trying to guide me. Experience has taught me that God asks four things: (1) that I keep in touch with Him through the Scriptures and prayer; (2) that I keep myself morally clean; (3) that I seek His guidance; and (4) that when He communicates, *I obey*. A breakdown in any one area on my part stops guidance.

I went to the church that night totally puzzled as to how the speech could help Kristian. In the middle of my prepared talk, I stopped and looked out over the audience.

"Something impels me to ask your prayers for a man who is to be executed tomorrow," I said. Then I told the story of Kristian. I saw a man rise from the audience and hurriedly go out the door.

After the speech I found him waiting for me. He was trembling as he said, "I must talk to you, Doctor Lundby!" He began by stating, "I know what hell is like, for I have been living there for many weeks."

This man, a quisling* during the war, was the only other person alive who was in on the bombing. He had testified falsely against Kristian and had helped Bakke escape. Would he be willing to sign a confession? Yes, he would. Anything to find peace of mind.

Even though it was late in the evening, I telephoned a friend in the High Court who referred me to the State Prosecutor. He was not at home. I called the chairman of our Parliament, but he thought I was some kind of a lunatic and hung up. In desperation, I had the quisling sign a confession which I personally left at the home of the State Prosecutor. The quisling gave me his address and agreed to appear at court in the morning.

Back in my room, I found myself terribly depressed. Should I go to the King? It seemed the only course left. I prayed for further help. Then, as I always do when at the end of my resources, I opened my Bible. In a few moments, I had my answer in these words from Proverbs:

*You are trying to get favor from a king, but a man's right is given by the Lord.***

This was God's way of telling me that I had done all I could, that He had taken over the case. I thanked Him and with a sense of release went to bed.

Events happened quickly in the morning. As soon as the State Prosecutor read the signed confession, he ordered a postponement of Kristian's execution. Then the quisling appeared and personally confirmed the facts about his signed statement.

Soon, legal machinery began to turn, which eventually led to Kristian's release. Kristian's conversion, by the way, was total and sincere, and we have kept in touch over the years.

This story is perhaps the most dramatic experience I have had

* Vidkun Quisling was a Norwegian fascist leader whose name became synonymous with "traitor." He was executed in 1945.

** Norwegian translation of Proverbs 29:26.

with guidance, but there have been many others which have made my life a continuous adventure. I will never understand why so many people try to rely on their own inadequate resources when the unlimited power of God is available to us—if we but ask for it.

Facing Death on the Atlantic

DWIGHT L. MOODY

WHEN about three days on our voyage, I remember, I was lying on my couch, as I generally do at sea, congratulating myself on my good fortune, and feeling very thankful to God. I considered myself a very fortunate man, for in all my extensive travels by land and sea I had never been in any accident of a serious nature.

Suddenly I was startled by a terrible crash and shock, as if the vessel had been driven on a rock. I did not at first feel much anxiety—perhaps I was too ill to think about it. My son jumped from his berth and rushed on deck. He was back again in a few moments, saying that the shaft was broken and the vessel sinking. I did not at first believe it could be so bad but concluded to dress and go on deck. The report was only too true. The captain told the affrighted passengers, who had rushed on deck, that there was no danger, and some of the second-cabin passengers returned to their berths, only to be driven out again by the in-rushing water, leaving everything behind them.

The officers and crew did all they could to save the vessel. But it was soon found that the pumps were useless, for the water poured into the ship too rapidly to be controlled. There was nothing more in the power of man to do. We were utterly, absolutely helpless. We could only stand still on the poor, drifting, sinking ship and look into our watery graves.

All this time, unknown to the passengers, the officers were making preparations for the last resort. The lifeboats were all put in readiness, provisions prepared, life-preservers in hand, the officers armed with revolvers to enforce their orders, and the question was evidently being debated in their mind whether to launch the boats at once, or wait. The sea was so heavy that the boats could hardly live in it. Two of the passengers had loaded revolvers ready to blow out their brains if the vessel should go down, preferring death by bullet to death by drowning.

At noon the captain told us that he had the water under control and was in hopes of drifting in the way of some passing vessel. The ship's bow was now high in the air while the stern seemed to settle more and more. The sea was very rough, and the ship rolled from side to side with fearful lurches. If she had pitched violently but once, the bulkheads must have burst, and the end come. The captain tried to keep up hope by telling us we should probably drift in the way of a ship by three o'clock that Saturday afternoon, but the night closed upon us without a sign of a sail.

That was an awful night, the darkest in all our lives! Seven hundred men, women, and children waiting for the doom that was settling upon us! No one dared to sleep. We were all together in the saloon of the first cabin—Jews, Protestants, Catholics, and skeptics—although I doubt if at that time there were any skeptics among us. The agony and suspense were too great for words. With blanched faces and trembling hearts the passengers looked at one another, as if trying to read what no one dared to speak. Rockets flamed into the sky, but there was no answer. We were drifting out of the track of the great steamers. Every hour seemed to increase our danger.

Sunday morning dawned without help or hope. Up to that

time no suggestion of religious services had been made. To have done that would almost certainly have produced a panic. In the awful suspense and dread that prevailed, a word about religion would have suggested the most terrible things to the passengers. But as that second night came on I asked General O. O. Howard, who was with us, to secure the captain's permission for a service in the saloon. The captain said:

"Most certainly; I am that kind, too."

We gave notice of the meeting, and to our surprise nearly every passenger attended, and I think everybody prayed, skeptics and all.

With one arm clasping a pillar to steady myself on the reeling vessel, I tried to read the ninety-first Psalm; and we prayed that God would still the raging of the sea and bring us to our desired haven. It was a new psalm to me from that hour. The eleventh verse touched me very deeply. It was like a voice of divine assurance, and it seemed a very real thing as I read: "He shall give his angels charge over thee, to keep thee in all thy ways." Surely He did it. I read also from Psalm 107:20–31. One lady thought those words must have been written for the occasion and afterward asked to see the Bible for herself. A German translated verse by verse as I read, for the benefit of his countrymen.

I was passing through a new experience. I had thought myself superior to the fear of death. I had often preached on the subject and urged Christians to realize this victory of faith. During the Civil War I had been under fire without fear. I was in Chicago during the great cholera epidemic and went around with the doctors visiting the sick and dying. Where they could go to look after the *bodies* of men, I said I could go to look after their *souls*. I remember a case of smallpox where the flesh had literally dropped away from the backbone, yet I went to the bedside of that poor sufferer again and again, with Bible and prayer, for Jesus' sake. In all this I had no fear of death.

But on the sinking ship it was different. There was no cloud between my soul and my Savior. I knew my sins had been put away and that if I died there it would be only to wake up in heaven. That was all settled long ago. But as my thoughts went out to my loved ones at home—my wife and children, my friends on both sides of the sea, the schools and all the interests so dear to me—and as I realized that perhaps the next hour would separate me forever from all these, so far as this world was concerned, I confess it almost broke me down. It was the darkest hour of my life!

I could not endure it. I must have relief, and relief came in prayer. God heard my cry, and enabled me to say, from the depth of my soul: "Thy will be done!" Sweet peace came to my heart. Let it be "Northfield or Heaven," it made no difference now. I went to bed and almost immediately fell asleep, and never slept more soundly in all my life. Out of the depths I cried unto the Lord, and He heard me and delivered me from all my fears. I can no more doubt that God gave answer to my prayer for relief than I can doubt my own existence.

About three o'clock at night I was aroused from my sound sleep by the voice of my son. "Come on deck, Father," he said. I followed him, and he pointed to a far-off light, rising and sinking on the sea. It was a messenger of deliverance to us. It proved to be the light of the steamer *Lake Huron,* whose lookout had seen our flaming signals of distress and supposed it was a vessel in flames. Oh, the joy of that moment, when those seven hundred despairing passengers beheld the approaching ship! Who can ever forget it?

But now the question was, Can this small steamer tow the helpless *Spree* a thousand miles to Queenstown? Every moment was watched with the intensest anxiety and prayer. It was a brave and perilous undertaking. The two vessels were at last connected by two great cables. If a storm arose these would snap like thread, and we must be left to our fate. But I had no fear. God would finish the work He had begun. The waves were calmed; the cables held; the steamer moved in the wake of the *Huron*. There were storms all about us, but they came not nigh our broken ship. Seven days after the accident, by the good hand of our God upon us, we were able to hold a joyous thanksgiving service in the harbor of Queenstown. The rescuing ship that God sent to us in our distress had just sufficient power to tow our ship and just enough coal to take her into port! Less would have been insufficient. Her captain also is a man of prayer, and he besought God's help to enable them to accomplish their dangerous and difficult task. God answered the united prayer of the distressed voyagers and brought them to their desired haven.

Am I My Brother's Keeper?

CECIL COFFEY

ONE DAY during the furious fighting on Okinawa in World War II, Desmond Doss stood beside a 77th Infantry Division lieutenant who was saying to his platoon, "Men, Doss is going to say a prayer before we go back on the lines."

Doss, a shy-looking young medical aid man, stepped forward, removed his helmet, and in a soft Virginia drawl asked God's protection on the platoon.

Nobody laughed. Nobody questioned the act. Instead, every man present breathed a thankful sigh. "The Preacher" was going along! And having "the Preacher" around when things got hot was mighty comforting.

Amazingly, the platoon came through that action without a single casualty. In a matter of minutes, word of the battlefield miracle flashed to the battalion commander and on to regimental and division levels. Hard-bitten colonels and generals pursed their lips in wonderment. Who was this praying medic, anyway?

"The Preacher" was listed in Army records as a private first class who hailed from Lynchburg, Virginia. He had a 1-A-O classification, which meant he was a conscientious objector who would *serve* in combat, but who would not *do* combat. His buddies gave him the clerical tag because he was about the oddest soldier they'd met: he didn't smoke and drink, never played cards, didn't curse, and was all the time leafing through a small Bible he carried in his jacket pocket. And, of course, he never carried a gun. That, in the opinion of the infantrymen, was not only odd—it was downright foolhardy!

But their opinion changed when they saw "the Preacher" go into action. In his year and three months of Pacific combat, the mild-mannered medic performed so many feats of single-handed heroism that his name became a symbol for gallantry throughout the 77th Division.

The most amazing feat of all occurred on April 29, 1945. It was Saturday. Doss, a Seventh-day Adventist, had been given permission to spend Saturdays in private worship. He had done so at Guam, Leyte, and Okinawa—until this Saturday when his company was ordered to assault a jagged escarpment ranging from seventy-five feet to four hundred feet high. There would be heavy casualties, and the company commander, looking around, found only one medical aid man fit for action.

"How about it, Doss? Men die on Saturday, too."

"It's all right with me, sir. Only—"

"Only what, Doss?'

"May I have a few more minutes with my Bible?"

The assault was delayed while Doss retired to a foxhole to pray. He prayed for ten minutes. Then he strapped on his medical equipment and climbed the cliff with his buddies.

"As our troops gained the summit," the Army record reads, "a heavy concentration of artillery, mortar, and machine-gun fire crashed into them, inflicting approximately seventy-five casualties and driving the others back."

The survivors climbed back down the cliff, regrouped at the bottom, and counted heads. Doss was among the missing. Then somebody shouted and pointed to the escarpment.

There, high above them, stood "the Preacher." He was waving frantically for a rope with which to lower the wounded. All about him were angry bursts of mortars and blasts of artillery.

The company commander ordered him down. Doss refused, again signaling for a rope. There was nothing to do but help him.

Meanwhile, the Japanese drew closer on the other side of the narrow summit. They started tossing grenades at Doss as he dashed here and there, tying tourniquets and giving plasma.

The Japanese made several attempts to overrun the top of the ridge, but they were stopped by grenade barrages from Doss's buddies, who had climbed back up to a ledge just under the escarpment crest.

For three sweating, concussion-rocked hours the slender medic tugged and hauled wounded men to the edge of the escarpment and lowered them—one by one—down the face of the cliff to friendly hands. Finally, the last man was lowered, and Doss slipped wearily down himself. There was something akin to reverence in the way his officers and buddies greeted him.

Five months later, the young medic stood on the lawn of the White House while President Truman placed the blue-ribboned Congressional Medal of Honor around his neck. Cameras clicked and reporters swarmed about him. Here was a story with a brand-new twist. For the first time in United States history, the nation had bestowed its highest military decoration on a conscientious objector!

Doss did not like the term "conscientious objector." He much preferred "conscientious cooperator." And who can deny that the latter term was the most apt?

Long before that bloody battle on Okinawa, Desmond Doss had answered the question "Am I my brother's keeper?" He had found a wider circle of love and service that categorized no man except as brother.

Doss, being a Christian, often turned the pages of his small Bible to favorite passages. One of these was John 14:15. Recorded in this passage are the words of Jesus, "If ye love me, keep my commandments." Doss correctly interpreted this to mean that love for God also means love for man, and love is measured by how man relates himself both to divinity and to humanity.

But what if Doss had been called upon to serve the enemy? Would there have been a difference? Would there have been the same obligation, in his mind, that there was when he saw his fellow soldiers fall during the battle for the Okinawan cliff?

Doss probably did not have to answer that question. But if it had been put to him, very likely he would have referred to remarks made by Jesus Christ nearly two thousand years before: "But I say unto you, Love your enemies, bless them that curse you, do good to them that hate you, and pray for them which despitefully use you, and persecute you" (Matthew 5:44).

The Ice-Pan Adventure

SIR WILFRED GRENFELL

ON EASTER Sunday, the 21st of April, 1908, it was still winter with us in Northern Newfoundland. Everything was covered with snow and ice. I was returning to the hospital after morning service when a boy came running over with the news that a large team of dogs had come from sixty miles to the southward to get a doctor to come at once on an urgent case. A fortnight before we had operated on a young man for acute bone disease of the thigh; but when he was sent home, the people had allowed the wound to close, and poison matter had accumulated. As it seemed probable that we should have to remove the leg, there was no time to be lost, and I therefore started immediately, the messengers following me with their team.

My dogs were especially good ones and had pulled me out of many a previous scrape by their sagacity and endurance. Moody, Watch, Spy, Doc, Brin, Jerry, Sue, and Jack were as beautiful beasts as ever hauled a komatik over our Northern barrens. The messengers had been anxious that their team should travel back with mine, for their animals were slow at best, and moreover were now tired from their long journey. My dogs, however, were so powerful that it was impossible to hold them back, and though I twice managed to wait for the following sledge, I had reached a village twenty miles to the south and had already fed my team when the others caught up.

That night the wind came in from sea, bringing with it both fog and rain, softening the snow and making the travelling very difficult. Besides this a heavy sea began heaving into the bay on the shores of which lay the little hamlet where I spent my first night. Our journey the next day would be over forty miles, the first ten lying on an arm of the sea.

In order not to be separated too long from my friends I sent them ahead of me by two hours, appointing as a rendezvous the log tilt on the other side of the bay. As I started the first rain of the year began to fall, and I was obliged to keep on what we call the "ballicaters," or ice barricades, for a much longer distance up the bay than I had anticipated. The sea, rolling in during the previous night, had smashed the ponderous layer of surface ice right up to the landwash. Between the huge ice-pans were gaping chasms, while half a mile out was all clear water.

Three miles from the shore is a small island situated in the middle of the bay. This had preserved an ice bridge, so that by crossing a few cracks I managed to get to it safely. From that point it was only four miles to the opposite shore, a saving of several miles if one could make it, instead of following the landwash around the bay. Although the ice looked rough, it seemed good, though one could see that it had been smashed up by the incoming sea and packed in tight again by the easterly wind. Therefore, without giving the matter a second thought, I flung myself on the komatik and the dogs started for the rocky promontory some four miles distant.

All went well till we were within about a quarter of a mile of our objective point. Then the wind dropped suddenly, and I noticed simultaneously that we were travelling over "sish" ice. By stabbing down with my whip-handle I could drive it through the thin coating of young ice which had formed on the surface. "Sish" ice is made up of tiny bits formed by the pounding together of the large pans by the heavy seas. So quickly had the wind veered and come offshore, and so rapidly did the packed slob, relieved of the inward pressure of the easterly breeze, "run abroad," that already I could not see any pan larger than ten feet square. The whole field of ice was loosening so rapidly that no retreat was possible.

There was not a moment to lose. I dragged off my oilskins and threw myself on my hands and knees beside the komatik so as to give a larger base to hold, shouting at the same time to my team to make a dash for the shore. We had not gone twenty yards when the dogs scented danger and hesitated, and the komatik sank instantly into the soft slob. Thus the dogs had to pull much harder, causing them to sink also.

It flashed across my mind that earlier in the year a man had been drowned in this same way by his team tangling their traces around him in the slob. I loosened my sheathknife, scrambled forward and cut the traces, retaining the leaders' trace wound securely round my wrist.

As I was in the water I could not discern anything that would bear us up, but I noticed that my leading dog was wallowing about near a piece of snow, packed and frozen together like a huge snowball, some twenty-five yards away. Upon this he had managed to scramble. He shook the ice and water from his shaggy coat and turned around to look for me. Perched up there out of the frigid water he seemed to think the situation the most natural in the world, and the weird black marking of his face made him appear to be grinning with satisfaction. The rest of us were bogged like flies in treacle.

Gradually I succeeded in hauling myself along by the line which was still attached to my wrist, and was nearly up to the snow-raft, when the leader turned adroitly round, slipped out of his harness, and once more leered at me with his grinning face.

There seemed nothing to be done, and I was beginning to feel drowsy with the cold when I noticed the trace of another dog near by. He had fallen through close to the pan, and was now unable to force his way out. Along his line I hauled myself, using him as a kind of bow anchor—and I soon lay, with my dogs around me, on the little island of slob ice.

The piece of frozen snow on which we lay was so small that it was evident we must all be drowned if we were forced to remain on it as it was driven seaward into open water. Twenty yards away was a larger and firmer pan floating in the sish, and if we could reach it I felt that we might postpone for a time the death which seemed inescapable. To my great satisfaction I now found that my hunting-knife was still tied on to the back of one of the dogs, where I had attached it when we first fell through. Soon the sealskin traces hanging on the dogs' harnesses were cut and spliced together to form one long line. I divided this and fastened the ends to the backs of my two leaders, attaching the two ends to my own wrists. My long sealskin boots, reaching to my hips, were full of ice and water, and I took them off and tied them separately on the dogs' backs. I had already lost my coat, cap, gloves and overalls.

Nothing seemed to be able to induce the dogs to move, even though I kept throwing them off the ice into the water. Perhaps it was only natural that they should struggle back, for once in the water they could see no other pan to which to swim. It flashed into my mind that my small black spaniel which was with me was as light as a feather and could get across with no difficulty. I showed him the direction and then flung a bit of ice towards the desired goal. Without a second's hesitation he made a dash and reached the pan safely, as the tough layer of sea ice easily carried his weight. As he lay on the white surface looking like a round black fuzz ball, my leaders could plainly see him. They now understood what I wanted and fought their way bravely towards the little spaniel, carrying with them the line that gave me yet another chance for my life. The other dogs followed them, and all but one succeeded in getting out on the new haven of refuge.

Taking all the run that the length of my little pan would

afford, I made a dive, slithering along the surface as far as possible before I once again fell through. This time I had taken the precaution to tie the harnesses under the dogs' bellies so that they could not slip them off, and after a long fight I was able to drag myself onto the new pan.

Though we had been working all the while towards the shore, the offshore wind had driven us a hundred yards farther seaward. On closer examination I found that the pan on which we were resting was not ice at all, but snow-covered slob, frozen into a mass which would certainly eventually break up in the heavy sea, which was momentarily increasing as the ice drove offshore before the wind. The westerly wind kept on rising—a bitter blast with us in winter, coming as it does over the Gulf ice.

Some yards away I could see my komatik with my thermos bottle and warm clothing on it, as well as matches and wood. In the memory of the oldest inhabitant no one had ever been adrift on the ice in this bay, and unless the team which had gone ahead should happen to come back to look for me, there was not one chance in a thousand of my being seen.

To protect myself from freezing I now cut down my long boots as far as the feet, and made a kind of jacket, which shielded my back from the rising wind.

By midday I had passed the island to which I had crossed on the ice bridge. The bridge was gone, so that if I did succeed in reaching that island I should only be marooned there and die of starvation. Five miles away to the north side of the bay the immense pans of Arctic ice were surging to and fro in the ground seas and thundering against the cliffs. No boat could have lived through such a surf, even if I had been seen from that quarter. Though it was hardly safe to move about on my little pan, I saw that I must have the skins of some of my dogs, if I were to live the night out without freezing. With some difficulty I now succeeded in killing three of my dogs—and I envied those dead beasts whose troubles were over so quickly. I questioned if, once I passed into the open sea, it would not be better to use my trusty knife on myself than to die by inches.

But the necessity for work saved me from undue philosophizing; and night found me ten miles on my sea-ward voyage, with the three dogs skinned and their fur wrapped around me as a coat. I also frayed a small piece of rope into oakum and mixed it with the fat from the intestines of my dogs. But, alas, I found that the matches in my box, which was always chained to me, were soaked to a pulp and quite useless. Had I been able to make a fire out there at sea, it would have looked so uncanny that I felt sure that the fishermen friends, whose tiny light I could just discern twinkling away in the bay, would see it. The carcasses of my dogs I piled up to make a wind-break, and at intervals I took off my clothes, wrung them out, swung them in the wind, and put on first one and then the other inside, hoping that the heat of my body would thus dry them. My feet gave me the most trouble, as the moccasins were so easily soaked through in the snow. But I remembered the way in which the Lapps who tended our reindeer carried grass with them, to use in their boots in place of dry socks. As soon as I could sit down I began to unravel the ropes from the dogs' harnesses, and although by this time my fingers were more or less frozen, I managed to stuff the oakum into my shoes.

Shortly before I had opened a box containing some old football clothes which I had not seen for twenty years. I was wearing this costume at the time; and though my cap, coat, and gloves were gone, as I stood there in a pair of my old Oxford University running shorts, and red, yellow and black Richmond football stockings, and a flannel shirt, I remembered involuntarily the little dying girl who asked to be dressed in her Sunday frock so that she might arrive in heaven properly attired.

Forcing my biggest dog to lie down, I cuddled up close to him, drew the improvised dogskin rug over me, and proceeded to go to sleep. One hand, being against the dog, was warm, but the other was frozen, and about midnight I woke up shivering enough, so I thought, to shatter my frail pan to atoms. The moon was just rising, and the wind was steadily driving me towards the open sea. Suddenly what seemed a miracle happened, for the wind veered, then dropped away entirely, leaving it flat calm. I turned over and fell asleep again. I was next awakened by the sudden and persistent thought that I must have a flag, and accordingly set to work to disarticulate the frozen legs of my dead dogs. Cold as it was I determined to sacrifice my shirt to top this rude flagpole as soon as the daylight came. When the legs were at last tied together with bits of old harness rope, they made the crookedest flagstaff that it has ever been my lot to see. Though with the rising of the sun the frost came out of the dogs' legs to some extent and the friction of waving it made the odd pole almost tie itself in knots, I could raise it three or four feet above my head, which was very important.

Once or twice I thought that I could distinguish men against the distant cliffs—for I had drifted out of the bay into the sea—but the objects turned out to be trees. Once also I thought that I saw a boat appearing and disappearing on the surface of the water, but it proved to be only a small piece of ice bobbing up and down. The rocking of my cradle on the waves had helped me to sleep, and I felt as well as I ever did in my life. I was confident that I could last another twenty-four hours if my boat would only hold out and not rot under the sun's rays. I could not help laughing at my position, standing hour after hour waving my shirt at those barren and lonely cliffs; but I can honestly say that from first to last not a single sensation of fear crossed my mind.

My own faith in the mystery of immortality is so untroubled that it now seemed almost natural to be passing to the portal of death from an ice-pan. Quite unbidden, the words of the old hymn kept running through my head:

My God, my Father, while I stray
Far from my home on life's rough way,
Oh, help me from my heart to say,
Thy will be done.

I had laid my wooden matches out to dry and was searching about on the pan for a piece of transparent ice which I could use as a burning-glass. I thought that I could make smoke enough to be seen from the land if only I could get some sort of a light. All at once I seemed to see the glitter of an oar, but I gave up the idea because I remembered that it was not water which lay between me and the land, but slob ice, and even if people had seen me, I did not imagine that they could force a boat through. The next time that I went back to my flag-waving, however, the glitter was very distinct, but my snow-glasses having been lost, I was partially snow-blind and distrusted my vision. But at last, besides the glide of an oar I made out the black streak of a boat's hull, and knew that if the pan held out for another hour I should be all right. The boat drew nearer and nearer, and I could make out my rescuers frantically waving. When they got close by they shouted, "Don't get excited. Keep on the pan where you are." They were far more excited than I, and had they only known, as I did, the sensations of a bath in the icy water, without the chance of drying one's self afterwards, they would not have expected me to wish to follow the example of the Apostle Peter.

As the first man leaped on my pan and grasped my hand, not a word was spoken, but I could see the emotions which he was trying to force back. A swallow of the hot tea which had been thoughtfully sent out in a bottle, the dogs hoisted on board, and we started for home, now forging along in open water, now pushing the pans apart with the oars, and now jumping out on the ice and hauling the boat over the pans.

It seems that the night before four men had been out on the

headland cutting up some seals which they had killed in the fall. As they were leaving for home, my ice-raft must have drifted clear of Hare Island, and one of them, with his keen fisherman's eyes, had detected something unusual on the ice. They at once returned to their village, saying that something living was adrift on the floe. The one man on that section of coast who owned a good spy-glass jumped up from his supper on hearing the news and hurried over to the lookout on the cliffs. Dusk though it was, he saw that a man was out on the ice, and noticed him every now and again waving his hands at the shore. He immediately surmised who it must be; so, little as I thought it, when night was closing in the men at the village were trying to launch a boat. Miles of ice lay between them and me, and the angry sea was hurling great blocks against the land. While I had considered myself a laughingstock, bowing with my flag at those unresponsive cliffs, many eyes were watching me.

By daybreak a fine volunteer crew had been organized, and the boat, with such a force behind it, would, I believe, have gone through anything. After seeing the heavy breakers through which we were guided, as at last we ran in at the harbour mouth, I knew well what the wives of that crew had been thinking when they saw their loved ones depart on such an errand.

Every soul in the village was waiting to shake hands as I landed; and even with the grip that one after another gave me, I did not find out that my hands were badly frostburnt—a fact which I have realized since, however. I must have looked a weird object as I stepped ashore, tied up in rags, stuffed out with oakum, and wrapped in the bloody dogskins.

The news had gone over to the hospital that I was lost, so I at once started north for St. Anthony, though I must confess that I did not greatly enjoy the trip, as I had to be hauled like a log, my feet being so frozen that I could not walk. For a few days subsequently I had painful reminders of the adventure in my frozen hands and feet, which forced me to keep to my bed—an unwelcome and unusual interlude in my way of life.

In our hallway stands a bronze tablet:

To the Memory of
Three Noble Dogs
Moody
Watch
Spy
Whose lives were given
For mine on the ice
April 21st, 1908.

The boy whose life I was intent on saving was brought to the hospital a day or so later in a boat, the ice having cleared off the coast temporarily; and he was soon on the highroad to recovery.

We all love life, and I was glad to have a new lease of it before me. As I went to sleep that night there still rang through my ears the same verse of the old hymn which had been my companion on the ice-pan:

Oh, help me from my heart to say,
Thy will be done.

Out of the Dungeon

CATHERINE MARSHALL

IT WAS the year 1924. In a courtroom in the Midwest, the judge's voice was grave as he looked down at the prisoner standing before him. "I am about to sentence you to a major prison for the third time. I know you are sick. And I know that more punishment is not the remedy. But your record leaves me powerless."

And so "hopeless criminal" was society's judgment of Starr Daily. The verdict seemed justified. At sixteen Starr's only ambition had been to build a reputation as a dangerous man. He dreamed of the time when the police would refer to him with a shudder.

He achieved his aim by becoming the leader of a gang of safecrackers. There was no safe he could not open, no time lock he could not take apart. But finally liquor made him careless, and he was caught.

There followed fourteen years of penal farms, chain gangs, and two extended penitentiary sentences. Through all that time Starr's father never lost hope that his son might be redeemed from his life of crime. His best efforts failed. He lived to see his Starr reenter prison for the third time. Starr never saw his father after that. The brokenhearted man died with a prayer for his son on his lips.

In prison Starr made two futile attempts to escape. Then he evolved a plan to instigate a prison riot. The deputy warden was to be seized and used as a shield and hostage. A stool-pigeon betrayed the plan, and Starr was sentenced to the dungeon.

Most strong men could not survive "the hole" for more than fifteen days. American prisons thirty-five years ago could be grim and brutal places. It was winter, and the walls of the dank cell seeped moisture. At six every morning, the prisoner would be given a piece of bread and a cup of water. Then he would be left hanging in handcuffs for twelve hours. At six in the evening, he would be let down for the night and given another piece of bread and another cup of water.

Starr survived fifteen days of this. By the last day in the cuffs, he could no longer stand on feet black with congealed blood. That morning "the Bull"—the keeper of the hole—had to lift the almost-unconscious man into the cuffs.

For weeks after that, the prisoner was allowed to lie on the icy stone floor—emaciated, unspeakably filthy, near death. He lost track of time. Mired in the lowest hell imaginable, only hate was keeping him alive—hate for the Bull, hate for the deputy warden who had vowed that he would force Starr to crawl to him like a dog, begging mercy.

Then there came a moment when the man on the floor was too weak to hate. Through that momentary opening crept a strange new thought: *All of my life I have been a dynamo of energy. What might have happened if I had used that energy for something good?*

Then the thought faded. *It's too late now; I'm dying.* There followed a half-waking, half-sleeping state of unconsciousness: moments of delirium, times of awareness.

This was followed by disconnected dreams, like mists floating across the brain. Time was no more. The prisoner was aware no longer of the frozen stone floor, of his filth, or of anyone who came or went.

Finally, the dreams began to take on meaning, to become rational in form and sequence. Suddenly Starr seemed to be in a garden. He knew that he had been in this same garden before—many times in childhood. It was in a shoe-shaped valley surrounded by gentle hills. At one end of the garden a great white-gray rock jutted out. Then Jesus Christ, the Man whom he had been trying to avoid all his life, was coming toward him. Now He stood face to face with Starr, looking deep into his eyes as if penetrating to the bottom of his soul. Love of a quality that he had never before felt was drawing the hate out of his heart, like extracting poison from an infected wound.

With a strange clarity, one part of Starr's mind thought *I am submerged in Reality, I'll never be the same again, now and through all eternity.*

There followed another dream in which all the people Starr had ever injured passed before his eyes. One by one, he poured out his love to them.

Then all who had injured him appeared, and on them too he bestowed the love needed to restore and to heal. The love flowed from beyond him, poured through him in a torrent of caring and ecstatic gratitude.

When the prisoner returned to consciousness, the cell did not look the same. Its grim grayness was gone. For him it was illuminated with a warm light. His feelings too were different. The prison environment no longer had the power to give him pain, only joy.

The next thing Starr knew, the door opened and the Bull said in a tone of voice Starr had never before heard him use, "Are you hungry? I could steal a sandwich from the kitchen and bring it to you."

The prisoner stared in amazement. But he was even more

startled at his own reply, "No, don't do that. Don't risk your neck by breaking a rule for me."

It was the Bull's turn to be astonished. He went off wonderingly, came back with the doctor, and Starr was carried to the prison hospital. Through a swift and surprising series of events, prison doors swung open for Starr Daily in March 1930, five years ahead of the time set for his release.

Was his experience on the cell floor a hallucination? No, not unless we would call what happened to Saul of Tarsus a hallucination. The proof was the change in the man. He who had been declared incorrigible by penologists, was from that moment cured of all criminal tendencies.

Peter Marshall loved the man that Starr Daily became and delighted in telling his story from the pulpit of the New York Avenue Presbyterian Church in Washington. In 1954, when I was in Hollywood for script conferences on *A Man Called Peter*, I drove out to the Daily's home in Van Nuys, California, for an overnight visit with Starr and his wife Marie.

A tall spare man, graying now, Starr's face bears the lines of the long hard years. But flashes of dry humor, spoken in a Midwestern drawl, light up the face.

From this man who had only a sixth-grade education have come eight books. He has lectured all over the nation. His knowledge of the criminal mind has contributed to valuable rethinking of prison techniques. He has personally been the Holy Spirit's vehicle for the reclamation of scores of criminals.

Four-Footed Angel

OLIVE BROADWAY as told to ESTHER L. VOGT

COLD March showers sluiced into my face as I stepped from the warmth of the church and headed across the lot toward the parsonage.

Thursday evening's meeting of the women's missionary society had finally closed, and as the pastor's wife I was the last to leave.

My husband had gone to a general conference in Detroit, and the children and I were alone. I half expected to find the parsonage cloaked with night, for the hour was late and the children should have been in bed hours ago.

Letting myself in quietly, I was surprised to find the kitchen light still burning. Ted, our oldest, his dark head bent over his books, was studying at the table. He looked up as I came in.

"H'lo, Mom. Wet out, isn't it?"

"It's a wild night, all right," I said wryly, peeling off my dripping coat and boots.

He went back to his homework.

As I turned to leave the kitchen, I looked down. Then I gasped. Our huge mangy dog lay stretched out at Ted's side!

"Ted! What's Brownie doing in the house?" I demanded. "You know he's never stayed inside before!"

Ted glanced up from his book and shrugged.

"Why, he just wanted in so I let him in. Then I decided I might as well bring my homework down here."

Brownie wanted in! That in itself was utterly incongruous. For that matter, so was everything else about that dog.

Black, brown and smelly—and of an undetermined breed—he had wandered to the parsonage one day and simply decided to stay. He adopted our whole big family, and was fiercely protective of us in every way. In fact, he craved us so that he wanted to be where we were. Yet once we'd let him into the house he developed a peculiar claustrophobic streak. He would race in terror from window to door to window until we'd let him out. No amount of bribing or petting could persuade Brownie to remain indoors. Even the dreary drip-drip of rain from the eaves failed to lure him inside. He preferred the most inclement outdoor weather to being enclosed.

Until now.

There he was, lying calmly beside Ted in the kitchen like a very ordinary house dog.

I remembered his fierce possessiveness of us before. Our large, red-brick parsonage sprawled comfortably on a big grassy plot behind the church and opposite the public school. Children often cut across the church property and through our yard when hurrying to and from school. We didn't mind. In fact, they were our friends. Against our better judgment we often had report cards thrust at us even before parents saw them.

That is, until the dog came. He snarled viciously at anyone who dared cross our yard, especially if he were carrying something. A neighbor who always had come through with a lunch box was forced to reroute his way to work; and more than once the milkman had to ward off the dog's attacks. Yet Brownie always came when I called him off.

Still, with people dropping in at our parsonage at any hour of the day, I was afraid some day I wouldn't get him called off in time.

Once I even called the police and asked if they would come and take care of the dog. They promised to if I'd let them shoot him on the spot. Of course I refused.

The Humane Society?

"Sure, lady. We'll get him. But you gotta catch him and shut him up for us," they said.

Shut Brownie up? Impossible! One might as well try to imprison a victim of claustrophobia in an elevator! Until a better solution presented itself, he would have to remain with us.

And that's how things stood that wild, stormy night I came home from church.

Shaking my head at Brownie's strange behavior, I went down to the basement to bolt the door that leads to the outside. I came back up directly and retired to the living room with the paper.

Ted already had gone up to bed, and I decided to turn in, too. The dog still lay on the kitchen floor, his shaggy head resting on his front paws.

Better put Brownie out first, I thought as I entered the kitchen to lock the back door. Rain still drummed steadily against the windows.

But when I tried to get the dog out of the door, he refused to budge. I wheedled; I coaxed. I pushed and pulled. He remained stationary.

Going to the refrigerator, I took out a chunk of meat and tried to entice him to the door by dangling it in front of him. He still refused to move.

With a bewildered sigh, I picked up his hind end and yanked him toward the door, and out of it. Like quicksilver, his front end slid back in.

I grabbed his front end, and the back was in. His four feet seemed like a baker's dozen. Stubborn, determined, yet placid, the dog would not leave the house. Talk about Balaam's ass—I knew exactly how Balaam felt!

Should I call Ted to help me? No, the hour was late and Ted

needed his sleep. I decided to shut all the doors to the kitchen and leave the dog inside. Then I went wearily up to bed.

The next morning the dog reverted to his true nature and frantically tore his way out of the house.

A puzzled frown ribbed my forehead as I went down to the basement to turn on the furnace. What had made Brownie behave so strangely? Why had he been determined to remain in the house this one particular night? I shook my head. There seemed to be no answer.

When I reached the bottom of the stairs, I felt a breath of cold, damp air. Then a queer, slimy feeling swept over me. The outside door was open! Was—was someone in the basement?

After the first wave of panic had drained from me, my reasoning returned.

Someone had gone out of the basement!

Limp with the reality of that fact, I looked around. The windows were as snug and tight on the inside as ever. *Whoever had gone out of that door had been in when I had gone down to bolt it the night before! He apparently had heard my unsuccessful attempts to put the dog out and knew he had to come up through the kitchen and face the dog—or go out the door he had come in earlier.*

That smelly, stray pooch had known this, and God had used him to keep us safe.

I have always believed that God has a definite work for His holy angels . . . and that as His child I could lay claim to the verse in Hebrews 1:14: "Are they [angels] not all ministering spirits, sent forth to minister for them who shall be heirs of salvation?"

But His "ministering spirit" had a peculiar form that wild, stormy night. Instead of glorious dazzling wings, the Lord had given our guardian angel four stubborn, mangy feet!

My Grave Was Number 12

JONATHAN LEE as told to ED ERNY

OF ONE THING I am certain. Before I die, God has a work for me to do. I have known this ever since a summer day in 1950 when a Communist soldier jabbed a bayonet in my back and snarled, "March!" Our destination: a small cemetery with 11 freshly covered graves. Mine was to be number 12.

"God, if You are alive, now's the time to prove it," I prayed.

And He did.

When the Korean war erupted without warning on "Black Sunday," June 25, 1950, I was a student at Seoul Theological Seminary. I had been out of high school less than a year. The floor of the school auditorium, where 300 of us students had gathered for an emergency prayer session, shivered with each blast of heavy artillery gunfire. Nearby we could hear the lethal chatter of machine guns. Russian-made bombers filled the sky overhead.

I remember our prayer that morning because few of us had prayed that way before. It was a prayer of repentance for our failure to win all of Korea to Christ while we had the chance.

When we left the auditorium, the matting where we had knelt was wet with tears.

The principal dismissed school advising us to go home until further notice. I went to my room and got a red-covered Gideon Bible. Then I joined the great anonymous tangle of human life that clotted every highway leading south. The Han River bridge had just been blown up and with it a ghastly toll of human life. Newly orphaned children sobbed unheeded in the streets. Every face I saw wore a mask of bewilderment and horror.

Forty-eight hours later I was in Wonju, my home town in the bleak "potato province" of Kangwondo. The place was a scene of frantic activity. Word had been received that a contingent of Reds was moving in on the city. I saw people piling household goods on homemade carts. Others were frenziedly bundling up a few prized possessions. Everyone, it seemed, was leaving Wonju in a desperate mass exodus.

In the confusion I managed to locate my mother, two sisters and five-year-old brother. Father was away at work and we knew that waiting for him would be disastrous.

"Hurry," I shouted. "The Communists will be here any minute now. We must leave immediately."

While mother gathered some bread and rice, I changed shoes. The long hike home had left my flimsy canvas ones in tatters. Now I put on a pair of army boots a friend had given me.

While we traveled south, the Reds pushed on ahead of us along another route. By the time we reached Choongju, the city had fallen. We still could hear distant gunfire. Everywhere were abandoned courtyards, burning vehicles and small children wandering forlornly through the debris. Along the road were twisted bodies—grotesque aftermath of a brief but savage battle.

There was no longer any point in continuing our flight. The enemy was in front of us and behind us. We decided we would be safest away from the city.

Not far from Choongju we found a small village and a friendly farmer, apparently unperturbed by the war. He was in the middle of the wheat harvest.

"I'll tell you what I'll do," he said. "You work for me in the harvest and your family can stay in my home. I'll pay you your wages in potatoes."

We accepted his offer. We were in no position to bargain and, anyway, eating potatoes would be nothing new to us.

The following day an elderly gentleman, wearing the traditional white robe and small peaked hat of the Korean scholar, appeared at the door of the thatched farmhouse.

"Young man, you are a student from Seoul?" he asked.

"That's right, sir," I replied, puzzled that he should know me.

"I have just been elected mayor of the village," he went on, "and I need a secretary. You can serve me and also the Glorious People's Party. Of course, you'll be well rewarded."

There was a long silence while I wondered how I could courteously refuse his offer.

"I'm sorry, sir," I finally stammered, "you see, I'm a Christian. I don't believe in Communism."

The mayor smiled condescendingly. "Look, son," he said, trying to be patient, "this is the day of a new order. Your whole world is upside down. Now, be reasonable. Think it over. I'll be back soon and by that time I hope you're ready to make the right decision." He turned and left.

Two days later I was winnowing wheat in the courtyard adjacent to the farmhouse, when I was startled by a rough hand on my shoulder. I spun around and looked into the ugly muzzle of a Russian-made submachine gun. Above me loomed the stony features of a well-muscled North Korean sergeant. He wore a yellow khaki uniform and a large helmet. Behind him, eight of his comrades appeared, as if by magic. Quickly they entered the house, seized my mother, sisters and brother, prodding them with their rifles into the courtyard. I stood dumbfounded, wondering what all this could mean.

The big sergeant scowled at me. Then he smiled—a thin smile of contempt.

"Now don't beg for your life like a woman. You and I both know who you are and what you're doing here," he said.

"But I'm a student from . . ."

"Shut up! We know who you are. We caught 11 of your friends and shot them this morning. You are number 12. Now we'll see if you South Korean soldiers die like men or if you scream for your lives like women."

Suddenly the truth hit me with sickening force. A South Korean soldier! I looked down at my khaki army pants and my military boots. Changing shoes, I now realized, had been far from wise. And even my head was close-cropped in army fashion.

"I know I'm wearing army clothes," I pleaded, "but I'm a student from Seoul. Believe me . . ."

The sergeant curled his lips in a cruel grimace. "Hah!"

At that moment the farmer appeared. Taking in the situation at a glance, he stepped forward in a bold attempt to save my life.

"Sir," he cried, "this boy is my son. He doesn't even know . . ."

"Filthy liar!" One of the soldiers slammed the butt of his rifle into the man's mouth, kicking him as he fell in a writhing heap. "We are not stupid. We know who this man is. He came here on a secret mission. We stopped it. The Glorious People's Army knows everything. This fellow is a spy, a dirty dog!"

My sisters and brothers looked on in stunned silence. Mother opened her mouth to cry but no voice came. A soldier moved behind me, jolting his bayonet into my back.

"March," he barked.

As I walked, with the point of the bayonet stinging my back, the awful hopelessness of the situation swept over me. I had heard how, in the face of death, a man's whole life will pass before him. Now it was happening to me.

Scores of events from my childhood reeled across my brain like a crazy motion picture. I remembered the long cold days, never free from hunger. When there was no rice we had eaten potatoes; and when the potatoes were gone we had eaten grass until our skin and eyes turned a jaundiced yellow. I saw again the shrunken forms of my two younger brothers who had died of starvation.

I remembered my father, a pitiful, helpless alcoholic. One night he had stumbled into my room in a drunken rage and had thrown my textbooks into the mud. Poor father.

But most of all, I recalled my mother—her courage and unshakable faith in Jesus Christ. Year after year she had trudged through the rain and snow, selling her noodles from door to door in order to keep us alive.

One winter morning less than a year before I had followed mother to the little church where she went to pray.

"God, I don't care about my life," she had cried. "I only ask that you grant one desire. For 14 years I have prayed that you would make my oldest son, Jonathan, a preacher and a man of God."

In the half darkness of that simple chapel, listening to my mother pray, I had given myself to Christ. I told God I would preach.

Was this to be the end of mother's 14 years of prayer? Was I to be taken out and shot like a dog?

"Where are You, God?" I found myself praying, "Are You a living God? Did You hear my mother pray those 14 years? God, if You are alive, show me."

I must have repeated that simple prayer 50 times during the short march from the farmhouse to the outskirts of the village. And as I prayed a strange thing happened. With each word I felt a tingling, indescribable peace inch its way up in my heart.

We had come to a huge oak tree that stood like a gnarled sentinel at the junction of three paths on the edge of the village. The sergeant was moving to the left, along the road that led to the cemetery and the 11 new graves.

Then I saw him. Coming toward us from behind the oak tree was an old man and two Communist soldiers, evidently bodyguards. Somehow the old fellow looked familiar in his white robe and small peaked hat. I blinked. It was none other than the gentleman who had talked to me at the farmhouse two days earlier. Could this be God's answer?

"Mayor," I called out, fighting to keep my voice steady, "Mayor!"

The old man flushed with embarrassment at being hailed by a youth, obviously under arrest by the Glorious People's Party.

"Mayor, you know that I am a student from Seoul. You visited me two days ago and asked me to be your secretary. This sergeant says I'm a secret agent. He's taking me to kill me. If he's right, I'm willing to die, but if this is a mistake, tell him."

The sergeant looked his surprise. He stopped short, turned to me and then to the mayor. His face wrinkled into a puzzled expression.

The old man reached into his pocket and produced an official-looking identification card stating that he was the newly elected chairman of the local people's government. He handed the card to the sergeant.

"Comrade Chairman," said the sergeant, "what is it that you want?"

"Comrade," the mayor returned. "You have made a mistake. This boy is not a South Korean soldier as you suppose, even though he is wearing a military uniform. He is a student from Seoul. I know because he was recommended to me as a secretary."

I watched the blood creep up the sergeant's face. His nostrils quivered and two large veins stood out in relief against his neck.

With one motion he ripped away my thin cotton shirt. He ran his hands across my shoulders, evidently looking for the telltale crease left by an army rifle strap. Then he grabbed my hands, inspecting them closely.

"Take off your boots," he growled.

My hands trembled as I unlaced the cumbersome army boots.

The sergeant moved his thick fingers over the soles of my feet, feeling for the heavy callouses that would betray the tedious military marches. Nothing again.

"Mayor," he ended in exasperation, "if this boy turns out to be a spy it will be your responsibility." He repeated the warning three times. With that he shoved me violently towards the old man.

I felt my legs buckle. In an instant I was on the ground, my head between my knees. Tears came to my eyes, and a prayer forced its way to my lips.

"Oh, God," I cried, "I thank You that You are a living God. I thank You that You are a living God."

I do not know how long I stayed on my knees under the big oak tree, but when I looked up, I was alone. The soldiers were gone. The old man and his bodyguards were gone. I never saw the mayor again, and to this day I do not know how the old gentleman knew I was a student from Seoul.

Long months stretched into years before the bloody Korean struggle gave way to a restive peace. On three other occasions I was almost killed—once by a Red Secret Service agent and twice by South Koreans who mistook me for the enemy. When I refused to join the North Korean army, I was forced to flee for my life. A fugitive, I hid for several months in a muddy camouflaged pit.

But through it all the mysterious calm never deserted me. My God was alive! I had discovered it for myself that day under the big gnarled oak.

And I had learned with Charles Spurgeon that "God's man is immortal until his work is done."

Blizzard

ONA LACY HUNTER

WHEN I hear people say that God has changed—that He does not answer prayers in miraculous ways as He did in Bible times—I want to cry out in protest.

I am alive today as proof of a modern miracle.

The event that changed me—and my life—happened after my first term of teaching. Being adventuresome, I wanted something more exciting then life in my home town, so I decided to visit my brother John on his cattle ranch in Alberta, Canada, and see what I could come up with.

While there I read of a scarcity of teachers in Saskatchewan and decided that was for me. I enrolled at once in the University of Saskatchewan for the three-month refresher course that would give me a certificate to teach.

The position I coveted was in a little town 100 miles from my brother's place.

On a cold, gray-and-white afternoon in October I found myself at the end of the railroad with a 30-mile sleigh ride ahead of me the next day.

In the hotel that night at supper, I met a young man whose

direct blue eyes and clean-cut face showed intelligence and dependability. With his tall, lean body dressed in a blue woolen shirt, plaid mackinaw, and corduroy pants tucked in lumberjack boots, he looked as I thought a construction engineer should. I was surprised when he said he was a homesteader, working in the livery barn for the winter.

Being two lonely young people, we soon knew a lot about each other. But homesteader Steve shook his dark head over my plans for going on to my school the next day.

"It looks like a blizzard is brewing. If signs don't change by morning, you may be here awhile," he said.

I smiled in unbelief. My brother, who knew this country well, had said just before he had helped me on the train,

"Sis, you needn't worry about being delayed by a blizzard. Too early for a real one."

Besides, I had promised to be in the town to meet with the trustees.

"I must go," I told Steve.

"Not if it looks like a big blow, you won't."

I ignored this remark and switched the conversation back to homesteading.

Later, when I started to my room, he warned:

"Don't be too disappointed if you can't leave tomorrow. People out here don't take chances with blizzards."

I laughed softly. It was flattering that this young man liked my company so well he was trying to scare me into staying longer!

Eager to get started, I breakfasted early. Steve had told me that he would be busy with the office work and that another man would drive me.

Back in my room, I waited impatiently for the sleigh and driver. When a knock did come, I threw open the door.

There stood Steve.

"Still set on going today?" he asked.

"Of course," I replied. Something like pity softened his eyes.

"Well, I'm doing the driving. The boss meant to send a greenhorn of a kid who could get lost without a blizzard."

I thanked him, my heart doing a strange little jig.

"Now don't think I'd be starting if weather conditions didn't look better," he said. "It'll be an hour yet before I can pick you up."

When at last I did stand by Steve's cutter, wearing the big fur coat he had borrowed for me, I was so weighted down he had to help me in.

"That's a footwarmer under your feet," he said, tucking the buffalo robe about our knees. "Probably won't burn long. Couldn't find enough charcoal."

Driving slowly over the snow-packed trail, there were no sounds except the thud of hoofs and creaking of iron runners against ice. The prairie, bleak and desolate, had no landmarks—just an occasional white mountain of a strawstack in a fenceless field.

We were well on our way when Steve began glancing upward at the yellow haze spreading over the sun.

"Don't look so good," he said. "But I believe we can make it before any storm."

Misgivings began to overwhelm me. Maybe I hadn't been so smart after all. Steve's expression and silence grew more ominous as the cold and velocity of the wind increased.

Sky and earth soon merged in a grayish whiteness—ghostly, unreal. Waves of loose snow swirled about us. Frozen granules pricked our faces like hot needlepoints. The screeching, wailing wind was unearthly. It sounded as though thousands of demons had been loosed to jeer us. Steve urged the horses on—their heads invisible at times.

I cried out when a sudden blast of wind lifted the cutter and slammed it down. Steve stood, and asked for my woolen scarf, which he tied over the lower part of his face.

"Get down in the cutter," he commanded. "Keep your face covered." He pulled the robe over me.

I quaked from fear. *He'll keep hold of the lines until he freezes,* I thought. *How he must hate me now.*

Presently the robe lifted.

"We're off the trail. The horses are circling," Steve shouted above the wind. "I can tell by the different angles of the wind. I'll try to keep them from narrowing their circles as long as I can." The robe dropped.

I could feel his pulling and sawing on the lines. Then he stopped. I peeped out and saw the lines looped over the dashboard.

"Please," I called, "get under this robe." No heat was coming from the footwarmer, but the buffalo robe offered some protection. Stiffly he crouched beside me and tried to talk through chattering teeth.

"Don't know where the horses will end up. They're prairie-bred. We'll have to trust them."

Trust. The word stirred deep thoughts. As a child, I'd taken Christ into my heart and life. I had trusted Him then to answer my prayers and, somehow, He always had. Why not now?

Two Bible verses flashed through my mind: "Thou shalt decree a thing and it shall be established unto thee," and "Take thou words and turn to the Lord." These meant *pray.*

While the horses floundered in snowdrifts and the cutter lurched, I asked the Lord to save us.

Steve sat rigid and silent. That he should perish for showing pity to a willful stranger must be a bitter thought!

"Oh, God, let Steve live if I must die," I prayed desperately while the horses kept dragging the cutter to—only God knew where.

Suddenly the cutter shuddered and stopped.

"I guess they've quit," Steve said.

I couldn't answer. My heart was in my throat, but my lips still moved in prayer. "Please let it be shelter."

Steve scrambled out and started feeling his way forward along the side of one of the horses.

"It's a straw-stack," he shouted on his return. "It may be a chance to save ourselves." There was little hope in his voice. But I knew at once that God had led the horses there. My heart was warm with gratitude.

Steve unsnapped the traces from the single-trees and loosed the harness on the horses. Together we stumbled through the storm to the stack in front of the horses. He took the bridle bits from their mouths. Next, with the toe of his heavy boot, he cleared two places on the stack—one in front of the horses; the other a little to one side.

I had been ignorant enough to expect him to set the straw afire so we could get warm. But he explained that burning it would leave us no shelter.

"We'll dig in and get out of the worst of the storm," he said.

At the cleared place away from the horses, we began pawing the straw with gloved hands. Our numbed fingers made little headway at first; but the exertion soon warmed us, and we went faster. We pushed the loose straw behind us as we went. I kept repeating to myself, "For the Lord will help me" and "Call upon me and I will answer thee."

Inside the stack we were still conscious of the wind and freezing cold.

"Dig at the side but don't turn 'round. Keep moving forward," Steve instructed. When I'd pause a moment to rest, he set me back to digging.

Once I felt a blissful drowsiness and began to drift away to a green pasture where the sun was warm and birds were singing. Steve's pounding and pummeling brought me out of my lethargy.

"For God's sake, stay awake and dig," he said. "Once you give up, you're gone."

I went back to clawing straw and to praying, determined not to stop again.

Time dragged. Whiteness was everywhere in our pit. We were color-blinded. How much longer could we stay alive?

Then I realized Steve wasn't moving.

I beat and pulled at him. "Give me strength, Lord, to keep Steve alive," I prayed. "You've been with us this far. Don't desert us now."

Steve stirred. God had heard me again. But now Steve was the weak one. When fatigue threatened, I prayed harder.

"We might as well give up and die easy," Steve said finally. "We'll never get out of here alive."

No, No, I thought. *God is with us. All things are possible to those who believe.*

"Don't you believe God answers prayers, Steve?" I asked.

He didn't answer—nor move.

"Dig, pray, believe," I continued. "God has performed greater miracles to save people. He hasn't changed."

I wept in thanksgiving when I felt Steve go back to work.

Some time later Steve cried, "The wind's not coming through the straw behind us now. The blizzard's over! We can turn 'round and dig out."

When we crawled from our straw cave, the east was rosy from the travail of birth. A new day was being born and, miracle of miracles, we were alive to welcome it!

I wanted to stay on my knees in the snow until I poured out my gratitude but Steve pulled me up.

In speechless wonder we gazed at each other. I think we both knew that miracles had happened in our hearts as well.

Steve dumped the snow from the cutter and went for the horses. He said they had kept alive by milling around the stack and pawing out straw to eat. Steve warmed the bridle-bits by holding them over some burning straw before putting them into the horses' mouths.

I had lost all desire to go on to school, I now had more to live for than adventure, so I went back to the hotel with Steve. I left the next day for my brother's place a changed girl. Love had come to me on the wings of the blizzard—a greater love for my Lord, and a new love for Steve whom I married in April.

This is why I know that God can do the miraculous—even today!

A Gentleman in Prison

TOKICHI ISHII

I WISH to tell how my heart was changed through the power of Jesus Christ. When I was a child, my parents were poor and I attended school for only two years. Since that time, which is more than thirty years ago, I have scarcely had a pen in my hand until I take it up now to write this story of my life. It is impossible for an ignorant fellow like myself to write in any but the simplest way; so I shall attempt to set down simply and truthfully the things that happened to me from my childhood up to the present time and to tell how I came to believe in Christ. In order to do this, I shall have to expose my shame and confess all my wickedness. But I shall be content if some villain like myself shall be helped by the story of how I was saved through God's leading and the efforts of Miss West and Miss Macdonald, the two ladies who visited me in prison.

At one time my father was purveyor to the feudal lord of Hikone, but he was a very heavy drinker and often drank more than two quarts of *sake* a day. He finally failed in business, left Hikone and moved with his family to Nagoya. My mother was the daughter of a Shinto priest. I was the youngest of three children, but the other two died when I was quite young.

We lived very comfortably until I was four or five years old, but by that time my father had squandered everything on drink, and my mother was greatly distressed over household matters. She was devoted to me and often went without the necessities of life herself in order to provide for me.

When I was ten, I left school, and my mother told me of her troubles. "I do not know what to do about your father," she said, "and I want you to help me. When he leaves home in the morning, you must follow wherever he goes and keep him from drinking." I followed my father about and would pluck at his sleeve when he was passing a saloon. "Do come home with me," I would beg. "Mother is so worried about you." My efforts were usually in vain, and he was often picked out of the gutter and brought home by the neighbors long after midnight.

Then another misfortune befell the family. My mother was taken ill with a very bad fever when I was just eleven years old. My father took us both to the house of an aunt and then disappeared. My aunt was very poor, and my mother was worried beyond words at being deserted in this way. We could not even afford to have a doctor for her.

I had to do something to help support the family. So I shouldered a pole with buckets attached to each end, bought some sawdust (which we burned for mosquito smudge), filled my buckets with it, and peddled the stuff from house to house. With what little money I got I helped to keep the family and buy medicine for Mother.

A little later my father returned, and the three of us began life together again. Unfortunately everyone gambled in the neighborhood where we lived. Up to this time I had never been known to do a mischievous thing, but I was soon gambling with the rest of them. I began to need money; the little my parents gave me was not enough, and I began to steal.

My parents discovered my wrongdoing and thinking it was no longer good for me to be at home, they hired me out to a chinaware manufacturer. I could not stand the restrictions of a strange house, so I ran away and found other work. I tried one place after another but did not stick to anything. My parents were helpless and let me do as I pleased.

I finally began to wander about peddling chinaware and spent the money I made in gambling. For a time I was very lucky, but gradually I used up all my money and found myself in a sorry plight.

The advice of my parents and friends made no impression on me. I began to drink, to quarrel with my companions, and to frequent houses of ill-fame. I became utterly useless for anything and gave up all attempts to earn an honest living.

Just at this time a great earthquake swept over Gifu and Aichi prefectures, and after it was over, the lumber merchants were very busy selling timber to repair the damage. I found work at a large well-known firm. Every day customers came in large numbers to do business, and the amount of material handled was very great. I consulted with a pal and got away with considerable quantities without its being noticed. At last we made away with several hundred yens' worth of stuff at one time, and we were caught. Our master dismissed us but did not notify the police.

I was subsequently caught, however, and found myself in the police station for the first time in my life. I was scared to death. I whispered to myself that if God would only let me go back home I would never do wrong again.

While awaiting trial, one fellow, who had been in prison before, said to me, "Don't worry about a petty little crime like yours; cheer up!" Under such encouragement I soon forgot all about the terrors of the police station. I was just nineteen years of age at this time.

By the time I had been four times in prison, I was already a confirmed criminal. In a prison community our claim to distinction is according to the extent of our crimes. The greater the crime, the greater the honor, and men brag openly of the depradations they have committed. Under such influence I determined early in my career to commit a really big crime and qualify for distinction in prison society.

I began to lay plans for escaping. I managed to improvise a covering out of some oilcloth I had gotten from an accomplice in the tailoring department, and one rainy day I wrapped it about me and escaped through an emergency exit.

Almost immediately I committed a theft, and with the money I stole, made my way to Tokyo. I rented a house and set up a small hardware shop. One day I was arrested on suspicion, as I could not explain why I had so much money in my possession, and I was detained for ten days in the police station. I finally said I had got the money by gambling, and I was not questioned further. This experience taught me to be suspicious of all the people who came to the shop as I thought they might be detectives or policemen.

Within three months I was in the police station again.

I got five months in prison, but about forty days before my time was up, I had a fight with one of the inmates and six months were added to my sentence. During this time my father died, and my old mother was left alone. Well did I know that she was awaiting the return of her wayward son, counting off the days on her fingers until I should come back to her repentant, and yet I cared nothing for her suffering, and continued in my wrongdoing.

When I came out, I returned home, and, without consulting my mother, ransomed a prostitute and made her my wife. I straightened up, however, and started watchmaking, a trade I had learned in prison; and my mother, my wife and I lived happily for nearly three years, although we had very little to live on.

All went well for a time, until one day a man I had known in prison came to see me, and by way of celebrating we took a drink together and then another, and another, until finally the lure of the old life returned upon me, and I started in on a course of crime again. My wife advised me to get away from Nagoya and move to Tokyo. I moved to Tokyo with my family and opened a bakeshop, but I knew nothing of the business and soon failed. Then I met an old pal and fell into temptation once more.

I now abandoned my wife and aged mother, committed a burglary, was caught and sent to prison for eleven years. As I had given a false name, my family had no way of tracing my whereabouts. I learned long afterwards that my wife and mother went back to their old home where my mother died broken-hearted on account of her wayward son.

I was not at all repentant, and determined to break prison and escape. I got hold of a nail about an inch and a half long, sharpened it on the edge of a piece of earthenware, and made a gimlet with three turns in it. After twenty days' work I managed to bore a hole with it and break a lock. Three of us had planned to escape together, but the first was caught and our attempt came to nothing. I kept racking my brains to find some other means of escape. At last I succeeded in making a saw about three inches and a half long, smuggled it into my cell, and began to cut the bars of my window. When I had got the bars almost sawn through, the plot was discovered, and I was severely punished.

I should have repented and apologized to the officials, but I only got more desperate and paid no attention to anything that was said to me. I was being constantly punished for breaking rules. I thought all restraint was cruelty and was filled with hate against everyone. I could not even live in peace with the other inmates but quarreled and fought with them. Finally I was put into solitary confinement.

My solitary confinement had the effect of making me still more stubborn and unmanageable. I cursed my jailors, fought with them, smashed the furniture in my cell, and altogether acted like a madman. Out of my eleven years' imprisonment I was at least half the time in solitary confinement, and I do not remember how many times I was punished otherwise.

One day when I had been in prison about seven years, I got angry with an official and attacked him. For this I was gagged, my hands bound tightly behind me, and my body suspended so that my toes barely reached the ground.

During this period, the vice-governor of the prison was said to be a Christian and had the reputation of being very kind. One day he came to my cell; and when he saw the plight I was in, he sent away the official in charge, untied the rope by which I was suspended, and let me down. He took the towel that was hanging at my belt and wiped the perspiration from my face. Before I knew it, the tears were rolling down my cheeks. That anyone should treat a hardened criminal like myself with such kindness was more than I could bear, and from that time forward I was a completely changed man.

Three years before my time was up, I received a good conduct badge from the prison governor, and made up my mind to reform when I was released. I decided to use the money I should receive from my prison work to start me in some honest business.

When I was leaving the prison, I was given four or five letters that an old pal of mine had sent. I had intended to return to my home at once, but after reading the letters I decided to go to see this friend first.

I went to Tokyo and saw this friend, and we talked about the days we had been together in prison and of the things that had happened after he left. He told me the whereabouts of another pal who had been a former accomplice, and I thought I would drop in on him also, and then go back to my own home in Nagoya.

This man, whose name was Sekiguchi, had been in the same workshop with me in Chiba prison. We talked an hour or more, and then my friend turned to me and said, "Ishii San, where are you thinking of going now?" I told him I had made up my mind to behave myself and go back to my own home at once. "I am glad to hear that you have reformed and that you are going home," said he, "but it is raining now and getting late, so you had better stop with me over night and start on your journey in the morning." I consented, and that night we went out and had a drink together. Sekiguchi said to me, "Ishii San, if you have made up your mind to reform, it really makes no difference whether you stay in Tokyo or go back to your own home. If you decide to stay in Tokyo, you can count on me to help you."

I was easily persuaded, and within a week he had found a house for me and I set up a small cake shop. During the next four months Sekiguchi and I met often, drank together, talked of the old times, and before long we began to hatch new plots.

One day I was robbed of my money. In a fit of anger over the robbery, I sold out my little shop and decided to return to my home in Nagoya. Sekiguchi said, "Well, of course if you are bound to go, I can't stop you; but if you happen to get your hands on anything down in the country, send it on to me." I assented in words, but I had really no intention of continuing my wrongdoing after I returned home.

I arrived in Nagoya and went at once to the old neighborhood where I had lived thirteen or fourteen years before, but found everything changed, and no one who knew anything about my wife. I stayed at a hotel that night and in the evening visited the family temple. Later I got drunk, and in my drunkenness squandered half the money I possessed.

The next day I discovered where my wife lived, but when I went to see her, I found that she belonged to another man. She had not heard anything of me after I had been put into prison eleven years before and she naturally thought I was either dead, or had forsaken her. She had married again about three years before I turned up. She was very much astonished to see me, and she told me some of the things that had happened during my absence, and especially about my mother's death.

My wife was mine no longer, my mother was dead, so there was no one left in all the world who would ever give me a thought.

While I was in prison, I believed in a god called Kompira Sama. I decided to take a journey to Shikohu and worship at the shrine there. As I journeyed along on my way, I committed all sorts of crimes.

I got as far as Kyoto. By this time I had less than five yen left in my pocket, and I began to feel a little lonely. I then remembered that Sekiguchi had told me of a friend of his that lived in Osaka, so I made my way over there, and found the man living in a certain hotel.

Within a week my money was all gone, and I had to give up my idea of going to Kompira Shrine. I was weak willed, and wicked thoughts soon rose in my heart again. I then recalled that Sekiguchi had suggested that if I picked up anything on my journeys I might send it on to him. I got hold of some stuff, sent it by freight to Tokyo. I plunged into my old ways again.

Not long after arriving in Osaka I committed a burglary, assaulted the inmates and stole about thirty yen. It would have been difficult to account for having so much money on me when I had no visible means of support; so I laid in a small stock of cakes, carried them with me and made a pretence of being a peddling confectioner. I then set out from Osaka. Along the way I deposited a little money now and then in the post office savings bank, and took care to have the passbook always with me. In this way I hoped to allay any suspicions the police might have of me for the passbook would show that I was an honest man and saving money.

I gradually made my way to Amagi where I put up at a house where only filthy beggars stayed. I did not mind this myself; but when I went to the public bath, I was refused admittance on account of it. This led to a quarrel with the owner and his wife, which resulted in my being arrested and taken to the police station. Being an old hand I knew I must first of all establish confidence, and so I showed my post office passbook to the police. The scheme succeeded, and I was let off.

Although I had escaped the police, I still was very angry at the bath-house man and his wife for daring to refuse me admittance when I had money to pay, and I vowed to return some day and kill off the whole bath-house family.

After this, I went on to Kompira Shrine. I worshiped there, and then made my way back to Osaka. Here I started my criminal ways once more.

On the morning of the twenty-ninth of April I went to Yokohama by street car thinking to try my hand at something there. Somehow or other I did not feel in the mood for doing anything desperate, and I wandered about the town for a while and then started to walk back along the Tokaido railroad. About ten o'clock at night I got as far as Suzugamori and sat down to rest in front of a teahouse which was closed for the night. Just at that moment a young woman twenty-four or twenty-five years of age came in sight, walking along by herself. I was suddenly seized with an overmastering passion; and when I had taken a quick glance about to see that no one was in sight, I sprang up and seized hold of her. The girl gave a loud scream and shouted, "Murder! Murder!" To stop her cries I snatched the towel that hung at my belt, twisted it around her neck and dragged her forward a few feet. To make sure she would not raise her voice again, I kept tightening the towel, and finally she ceased to breathe. I then looked into the girl's kimono sleeve and found a purse containing about thirty-six yen and a small book which I took possession of, and escaped from the place.

Shall I not call myself the worst villain that ever lived? As I look back upon the self who committed that awful crime, my present self recoils in horror, and the hair of my body stands up on end at the thought of my terrible sins.

I returned to Tokyo to Sekiguchi's house and loafed about for four or five days as if nothing had happened. I began to think that if I fooled about much longer and did nothing, I might be suspected by the neighborhood. So I made a pretence of doing business but charged about ten percent less than the cost price in order to gain the good will of the people round about.

I broke into a certain house, bound the inmates, and tried by threats to force the wife to tell me where their money was. At this the man began to shout, "Thief! thief!" whereupon I seized a towel that was hanging in the room, and twisted it around his neck. The wife, seeing me do this, summoned up her strength and shouted with all her might, "Murder! murder!" At this I seized a narrow obi that was hanging in the room and strangled her also.

Just then I heard a voice from a neighboring house, and taking time only to seize the woman's gold watch which was lying near, I made my escape.

After leaving the house I walked along the Tokaido railroad for a while, broke into another house, stole some things, and sent them to Sekiguchi. At Iwabuchi I was walking along about midnight when a policeman suddenly appeared and stopped me. There seemed no way of escape so I went along, taking advantage of the darkness to drop my dagger by the side of the road. When I was examined at the police station, I showed my passbook and as usual was let off. I retraced my steps, picked up the dagger, and went on. As the night was very dark I stumbled and fell headlong into a river thirteen or fourteen feet below me. I broke a rib, but managed to crawl out as far as a strawstack in a nearby field; and lay there for three days and three nights unable to move, and without anything to eat or drink. I thought I should die, but I finally recovered, although I was not able to commit any more crimes for some time.

One night Sekiguchi and I went together to Fukagawa ward and attempted to enter a house. The servant was aroused, however, and began to throw things at us until we were obliged to flee. I was so angry that I determined to return some day and burn the house down.

After this it was not safe for either of us to go back to

Sekiguchi's house, and on the eighth of December we decided to start off together for the country. But the wrath of Heaven overtook us. That evening when we returned to our lodgings, five policemen were waiting for us.

I was put into a police cell with seven or eight other men who were talking among themselves about some murders that had been committed around Tokyo. This and that murderer had been arrested, they said, and among them they mentioned a man named Komori who was being tried for the murder of a geisha at Suzugamori. When I heard this, I said to myself, "How can they be trying Komori for this murder, when it was I who did it?" For a moment I doubted my own ears, but upon inquiry found that the man knew the facts, and that it was actually true that an innocent man was being tried for the Oharu murder.

I began to think. When I was arrested and sentenced for my crimes, I hated policemen and detectives, judges and procurators, and was always dissatisfied with the sentences I received, in spite of the fact that I really committed the crimes. What then must be the feeling and the suffering of this innocent Komori as he lay in prison for months, accused of a crime he did not commit? What about his family and relatives? I cannot express by word of mouth, nor in any shape or form, the agony that must have been theirs. I kept on thinking. After all, a human being must die once anyway, and so I decided to confess my guilt and save the innocent Komori. I decided that I might as well make a clean breast of all my crimes, which I did at once.

I was transferred to the prison where I am now writing this story, on the thirtieth of December, 1915. As I look back now, I see that all this was the working of God's providence. Of course at the time I knew nothing of God's heart, but I firmly believe now that God had already fathomed the depths of mine.

Let me now tell how I came to believe from the bottom of my heart in the teachings of Jesus Christ.

In order to atone for my sins, I had confessed everything, and I felt that my life was already ended. Day by day I sat alone in my cell with no one to talk to and with nothing to do. One night when everyone was asleep and the prison was silent, I suddenly wakened and began to think of all the unmentionable sins I had ever committed. I had given myself up to die when I confessed my sins, but now in the darkness I began to think of what would happen if I should die just as I was. Where should I go? Was there such a thing as a soul? I did not know, but if there were, must mine not go to Hell? Surely this was a dark future for me, and as I thought of it I was filled with an anguish I could scarcely bear. In the days of my strength, when I was concerned only with lust and money, such thoughts never entered my head; but now with certain death staring me in the face, my agony was heavier than I could bear.

The year 1915 closed and the first day of the New Year opened. Early in the morning a special New Year's meal was brought to me, and I was told that two ladies by the names of Miss West and Miss Macdonald had sent it. I had never seen nor heard of them before. I told the official that I could not accept the gift. The official said that these ladies were Christian missionaries, and had sent the food out of kindness and sympathy, and so I need not hesitate to accept it.

The food was sent to me during the first three days of the New Year. A few days later a New Testament and two or three other Christian books were received from the same source, but I put them up on the shelf and did not even look into them.

One day Miss West came to visit me and talked to me about Jesus Christ. Although I thought it was very kind of Miss West to come, I did not pay much attention to what she said. These visits continued from time to time.

One day I got tired of sitting with nothing to do, and I took the New Testament down from the shelf and glanced at the beginning and at the middle. I began to read:—

> And it came to pass, when the time was come that he should be received up, he stedfastly set his face to go to Jerusalem, and sent

> messengers before his face: and they went, and entered into a village of the Samaritans, to make ready for him. And they did not receive him, because his face was as though he would go to Jerusalem. And when his disciples James and John saw this, they said, Lord, wilt thou that we command fire to come down from heaven, and consume them, even as Elias did? But he turned and rebuked them, and said, Ye know not what manner of spirit ye are of. For the Son of man is not come to destroy men's lives, but to save them.

I laid the book down thinking that these were surely the words of some one who wanted to teach men the path of virtue, but otherwise I was not specially moved by them.

A little later I took the book down once more. This time I read how Jesus was handed over to Pilate by his enemies, was tried unjustly and put to death by crucifixion.

As I read this, I began to think. This person called Jesus evidently tried to lead others into the path of virtue, and it seemed an inhuman thing to crucify him simply because he had different religious opinions from others.

I went on, and my attention was taken by these words: "And Jesus said, Father, forgive them, for they know not what they do." I stopped: I was stabbed to the heart, as if pierced by a five-inch nail. What did the verse reveal to me? Shall I call it the love of the heart of Christ? Shall I call it his compassion? I do not know what to call it. I only know that with an unspeakably grateful heart, I believed. Through this simple sentence I was led into the whole of Christianity.

Today I am sitting in my prison cell with no liberty to come and go, and yet I am far more contented than in the days of my freedom. No matter what discomforts I endure there is only gladness in my heart.

I wish to speak now of the power of Christ. I have been more than twenty years in prison since I was nineteen years of age, and during that time I have known what it meant to endure suffering. I have passed through all sorts of experiences and have been urged often to repent of my sins. In spite of this, however, I did not repent, but on the contrary became more and more hardened. And then by the power of that one word of Christ's, "Father, forgive them, for they know not what they do," my unspeakably hardened heart was changed, and I repented of all my crimes.

My trial for the murder of Oharu dragged on for many long days and months, and I was finally acquitted in the first court. I was greatly disheartened about this for a time, for I knew that if I was acquitted, the innocent Komori would suffer the penalty.

By this time, however, I had faith in God, and so I reasoned it out in this way. The case will never be settled by man's power, so I must pray unceasingly that it be settled by the power of God. I knew that Miss Macdonald and Miss West were praying for me, and I believe God used their prayers to pierce through the heart of the judge; for in the appeal court I received the fair impartial judgment of God.

As I think it all out now I see that I am worse than a beast. The cat and dog are of some use to man. The wild animal of the mountain is useful when he is dead for his fur and flesh. I have not only been of no use to anyone but have done untold harm. I can compare myself to nothing but a tuberculosis germ; I have been but a plague to people. I feel ashamed to show my face. If there were only a hole somewhere, I should like to crawl in and hide myself. Nevertheless, when I realize that I have lived until today to receive the gracious love of God, there is nothing but joy in my heart. Whatever happens to me in the future, I desire only to do the will of Jesus Christ.

Notes Taken From Caroline Macdonald's Journal:

I saw him just two weeks after his writing was finished, and as it happened, for the last time. The day of doom is not publicly fixed in Japan, and neither he nor I knew that it would be the last time; but we both knew it might be, and we faced the issue. "I do not know when it will come," he said, "perhaps tomorrow, perhaps the day after; but I have finished my writing and my task is done. I am just waiting now to lay down this body of sin and go to Him." His face, marred and sin-stained as it was, was lit up with a radiance not of this world as he spoke of his going.

The story of his passing was told us afterwards by the Buddhist chaplain who was with him.

"Many who die on the scaffold face death with a firm resolution to win a good name for themselves at the end, and not to be a laughing stock to the world. But Ishii's fortitude was far different from that. He had not the slightest appearance of desiring to win a good name or of merely enduring the inevitable. With humility and great earnestness, he seemed to see nothing but the glory of the heavenly world to which he was returning, when he had cast off the heavy load of his sins; just as one turns with great yearning to his own native home. Among the officials who stood by and saw the clear color of his face and the courage with which he bore himself, there was no one but involuntarily paid him respect and honor. On the very scaffold, when in a moment his life was to disappear like a dewdrop, he uttered those last words of his: "My soul, purified, today returns to the City of God!"

Christmas Eve Miracle

ALEXANDER LAKE

ONE Christmas Eve, when I was a police reporter on the Seattle *Post Intelligencer,* I was idling at my typewriter in the police station press room when an overwhelming impulse sent me hurrying to Pioneer Square, three blocks down the street, where I arrived just in time to knock a loaded revolver away from the head of a man about to shoot himself.

A cold drizzle was falling, and the gun slid across the glistening path and came to rest in the grass. The little park was deserted. For an unreal moment, I stared at the illuminated hands of a clock in the window of a restaurant across the street. They read five minutes past seven.

Three or four minutes ago, I'd been half-dozing in the warm, poorly ventilated reporters' room. Now here I was at the foot of Seattle's Skid Row with a man I'd just saved from death.

Whence had come the impulse that sent me out into the dreary night? What had directed me to the exact spot where a fellow human was about to blast himself into eternity? It seemed so fantastic that I wondered if I was dreaming. However, I didn't have time to think much about it for the man suddenly dropped to his knees and began fumbling in the wet grass for the gun.

I pushed him with my foot, and he sprawled on his face. I picked up the gun and slipped it into my coat pocket. Then I helped the man to his feet. He was blubbering.

"Snap out of it, fellow," I said. "I'm here to help you. Let's go across to that restaurant and get some hot soup, or something."

He didn't answer. I put my hand on his shoulder.

"For God's sake," he said, "go away. Leave me alone." Then he covered his face with his hands.

Rain was running down the back of my neck, and I pulled up my coat collar. "Come on, Jack. Snap out of it," I said.

He looked at me. "You know me?" he asked.

"No."

"You called me *Jack.*"

"Okay, Jack. Let's go someplace where it's dry. Someplace where we can talk."

He shook his head. "I don't want to talk," he said. But he did want to talk, for words began pouring from him.

"I can't go on," he said. "I can't face them. They have no food. No Christmas presents. I'm tired and sick. I'm in hell."

"Who are they?" I said.

"My family. My wife and kids. I've walked these streets for six days with that stuff," he said, pointing to a square bundle lying on the walk. "Stuff to prevent windshields fogging," he explained. "I've been trying to sell it. Six days. Know how much I've made? Seventy-five cents."

"How about that soup now, Jack?" I said.

"Yes . . . Jack," he said bitterly. "Jack Bryan—Auto Accessories. Know what? The constable locked the doors of my business last week. Didn't even let me take the money from the till. Finance company took my car. No money. No food in the house. I picked up this line of windshield stuff to sell. Six days. Seventy-five cents. Going crazy with worry. I saw that gun in a service station and stole it. No food in the house. No money for rent. Six days . . ."

"Yes, yes, Jack," I interrupted—for he was becoming incoherent. He was cold and wet; probably hungry. I walked him across First Street to a restaurant.

We never did get that soup. Inside the restaurant, I went to a pay phone and called my city editor. He ordered me to rush over to the morgue and ride out with the "dead wagon" to pick up the body of a woman reported murdered.

Grabbing Bryan by the arm, I hurried him up an alley and into the morgue garage. Bill Corson, son of the City Coroner, was in the driver's seat. We piled in beside him and rolled out into the night.

Bryan didn't seem to know or to care what was happening. He sat there next to me, hunched and silent. I handed him two ten-dollar bills, but he pushed them aside, so I crumpled them and pushed them into the breast pocket of his coat.

Corson turned left beyond King Street station, and the wagon squished through mud and slush into Seattle's worst slum district—a section where poverty-stricken Italians lived in squalor. We pulled up before a ramshackle house overflowing with wailing, moaning neighbors. Corson and I carried the basket, and Bryan followed.

We set the basket on the floor in a small bedroom in which the body of a large, work-worn woman lay on a broken-down bed. She hadn't been murdered—she'd dropped dead at her washtub.

Corson ushered the neighbors into the yard. The woman's husband and five small children remained at the foot of the bed, clutching one another.

I'll never forget the misery in that husband's eyes. Bryan noticed it too, for as Corson and I lifted the heavy body into the basket, he walked to the man, and without a word, handed him one of the two ten-dollar bills I'd put in his pocket.

The husband sobbed, and the children began a sympathetic lament. Corson strapped down the lid, and we carried the basket through the mob of neighbors in the yard, and lifted it into the wagon.

As the three of us settled into the front seat, Bryan said, "I've got to get home. Please—take me home. I must have been crazy. I didn't know what misery is."

Corson swung around to James Street and dropped Bryan and me off in front of a small white cottage. Bryan hurried up the steps. I followed, slowly. I paused in the little hall and watched through the kitchen door. With eyes closed, Bryan was holding his wife as if he'd never let her go. Two little girls, about three and five years old, were each hugging one of their daddy's legs.

Then Mrs. Bryan noticed me and moved out of her husband's arms. She came into the hall and shut the door. "He's been so worried and sick," she said, eyes filled with tears. "Tonight when he wasn't home by seven o'clock, I knelt down and prayed God to please take care of him, and to bring him home safely. And here he is."

I realized then, why the impulse to get to Pioneer Square had come to me at exactly seven. I felt awed and humble.

"His business went broke," Mrs. Bryan said, "but I'm not a bit worried. I've asked God to take care of that, too."

I looked into Mrs. Bryan's calm eyes and thought: It was this woman's faith in God that sent me out into this dismal night to bring her husband home to her.

I said, "I'm certain things will work out just as you want them to, Mrs. Bryan."

I told her to call me at the police station if she needed me, then stepped out onto the little porch. As the door closed behind me, I remembered that Bryan had given ten dollars to the Italian, so I turned back into the house. Father, mother, and the two little girls were kneeling at kitchen chairs, praying. I stood for a moment, then tiptoeing to the table put a few one-dollar bills on it and slipped out.

God did take care of Bryan's business. Today, automobile men up and down the Pacific Coast know Jack Bryan and his line of accessories.

Back at the police station press room, I picked up the phone and called the city desk. "That trip with Corson," I said.

"I'll give you a rewrite man," said the city editor.

"No—don't bother," I said. "There wasn't any story."

Birth on Death Row

AGNES SANFORD

THERE LIVES in the deep South a little old lady who, being filled with the Spirit, goes forth to seek and to save those who are most truly lost. She is known in prisons and in poorhouses and in dives and in joints. She heard one day of a murderer—a multiple and confessed murderer—who was condemned to die. She went to see him. She knew that she could not save his life, forfeited to the laws of the land. But she could bring him out of that death of the soul which he had already suffered.

"You can't go in there, Miss Nellie!" said the guard, "He's dangerous. We never go into his cell alone—it takes two or three of us to manage him."

"He won't bother me," said Miss Nellie serenely.

"But alone—"

"I'm not alone," said Miss Nellie. And the guard, knowing what she meant, stepped aside and let her into the cell.

The great black man leaped from his bed, cursing and swearing and shouting.

Miss Nellie merely stood still and prayed for him, seeing with the eyes of Christ the real man behind the savage—the real man simple, childlike, capable of a great love and a real holiness. Because she could see the real man and because she poured out upon him the Holy Spirit of Christ—or, in other words, the love of God in action—he ceased raving after a while, at least long enough to draw breath.

"I understand," murmured the mother of many children and grandchildren. "I'm real sorry you have to go to State Penitentiary . . ." By which she meant, and he knew that she meant, to the electric chair.

"You don't understand!" roared the captive. "Nobody ever done understand me! My mother didn't and my father didn't and—"

"Jesus understands you," said Miss Nellie.

Whereupon the tormented man began once more to shout curses, shaking his huge clenched hands at the ceiling. "Don't give me none of that Jesus crap!" he yelled.

Not in the least intimidated, Miss Nellie simply stood there and prayed for him. Whether at this moment she was aware of feeling love for him I do not know, but I doubt it. My guess would be that she was, in her spirit, too truly *him* to feel anything *for* him in the conscious mind. This deep identification through the Spirit goes far beyond any detectable emotion. She was him and yet she was also herself praying for him, as an actor on the stage is the person whom he portrays and at the same time also himself interpreting that person to the audience.

After a while there was a brief silence. Then he cried out to her, "What's dat? What dat I feels? What's a-comin' all over me?"

"That is the Holy Spirit," said Miss Nellie serenely.

"But I'm happy! I never felt like dis in my whole life!"

"That's the joy of the Lord," Miss Nellie explained.

For an hour or more she sat on the crude pallet beside this man and told him very simply the story of the love of Jesus and of the Holy Spirit of Jesus, while tears ran down his cheeks and shouts of joy rang from time to time out into the corridors to the amazement of the guards and the other prisoners.

The next week she went again to see him. Before she reached the jail she caught sight of him looking out from behind the bars, his hands flung high in the air in praise. "He ain't left me yet!" he shouted to her. "He ain't left me yet!"

Before this man went to the electric chair he converted every prisoner on his corridor. The last man he converted was the executioner. For he walked to the electric chair in the glory of God as a man about to enter into heaven, which indeed he was.

"I'll never do it again," said the executioner. "I can't."

Return from Tomorrow

GEORGE C. RITCHIE, JR., M.D.

WHEN I was sent to the base hospital at Camp Barkeley, Texas, early in December, 1943, I had no idea I was seriously ill. I'd just completed basic training, and my only thought was to get on the train to Richmond, Virginia, to enter medical school as part of the Army's doctor-training program. It was an unheard-of break for a private, and I wasn't going to let a chest cold cheat me out of it.

On December 19 I was moved to the recuperation wing. A jeep was to pick me up at 4 A.M. the following morning to drive me to the station to catch the train to Richmond. About nine that night I began to run a fever. Three A.M.—I decided to get up and dress.

The next half-hour is a blur. I remember being too weak to finish dressing. I remember a nurse coming to the room, and then a doctor, and then a bell-clanging ambulance ride to the X-ray building.

The whir of the X-ray machine is the last thing I remember.

When I opened my eyes, I was lying in a little room I had never seen before. A tiny light burned in a nearby lamp. For a while I lay there, trying to recall where I was. All of a sudden I sat bolt upright. The train! I'd miss the train to Richmond!

Now I know that what I am about to describe will sound incredible. I do not understand it any more than I ask you to; all that I can do is relate the events of that night as they occurred. I sprang out of bed and looked around the room for my uniform. Not on the bedrail. I stopped, staring. Someone was lying in the bed I had just left.

I stepped closer in the dim light, then drew back. He was dead. The slack jaw, the gray skin were awful. Then I saw the ring, the Phi Gamma Delta fraternity ring I had worn for two years.

I ran into the hall, eager to escape the mystery of that room.

"Look out!" I shouted to an orderly bearing down on me. He seemed not to hear, and a second later he had passed the very spot where I stood as though I had not been there.

It was too strange to think about. I reached the door, went through and found myself in the darkness outside, speeding toward Richmond. Running? Flying? I only know that the dark earth was slipping past while other thoughts occupied my mind, terrifying and unaccountable ones. The orderly had not seen me. What if the people at medical school could not see me either?

Suddenly, one thing became clear to me: in some unimaginable way I had lost my firmness of flesh.

I was beginning to know, too, that the body on that bed was mine, unaccountably separated from me, and that I *must* get back and rejoin it as fast as I could.

Finding the base and the hospital was no problem. I seemed to be back there almost as soon as I thought of it. But where was the little room I had left? So began what must have been one of the strangest searches ever to take place: the search for myself. I ran from one ward to the next, past room after room of sleeping soldiers, all about my age. Several times I stopped by a sleeping figure that was exactly as I imagined myself. But the fraternity ring, the Phi Gam ring, was lacking, and I would speed on.

At last I entered a little room with a single dim light. A sheet had been drawn over the figure on the bed, but the arms lay outside. On the left hand was the ring.

I tried to draw back the sheet, but I could not seize it. I thought suddenly, "This is death." It was the first time I had connected death with what had happened to me.

In that most despairing moment, the little room began to fill with light. I say "light," but there is no word in our language to describe brilliance that intense. I must try to find words, however, because incomprehensible as the experience was to my intellect, it has affected every moment of my life.

The light which entered that room was Christ. I knew because a thought was put deep within me, "You are in the presence of the Son of God." I have called Him "light" for that room was flooded, pierced, illuminated, by the most total compassion I have ever felt. It was a presence so comforting, so joyous and all-satisfying, that I wanted to lose myself forever in its wonder.

With the presence of Christ (simultaneously, though I must tell it one by one) also had entered every single episode of my entire life. There was no first or last, each one was contemporary, each one asked a single question, "What did you do with your time on earth?"

I looked anxiously among the scenes before me: school, home, scouting and the cross-country track team—a fairly typical boyhood, yet in the light of that presence it seemed a trivial existence.

"Did you tell anyone about Me?" came the question.

"I didn't have time," I answered. "I was planning to, then this happened. I'm too young to die!"

"No one," the thought was inexpressibly gentle, "is too young."

A new wave of light spread through the room and suddenly we were in another world. Or rather, I perceived, a very different world occupying the same space. I followed Christ through ordinary streets and countrysides thronged with people. People with the unhappiest faces I ever have seen. I saw businessmen walking the corridors of the places where they had worked, trying vainly to get someone to listen to them. I saw a mother following a 60-year-old man, her son I guessed, cautioning him, instructing him. He did not seem to be listening.

Suddenly I was remembering myself, that very night, caring about nothing but getting to Richmond. Was it the same for these people; had their hearts and minds been all concerned with earthly things, and now, having lost earth, were they still fixed hopelessly here? I wondered if this was hell. To care most when you are most powerless; this would be hell indeed.

I was permitted to look at two more worlds that night—I cannot say "spirit worlds" for they were too real, too solid. Both were introduced the same way; a new quality of light, a new openness of vision, and suddenly it was apparent what had been there all along. The second world, like the first, occupied this very surface of the earth, but it was a vastly different realm. Here was no absorption with earthly things, but—for want of a better word to sum it up—with truth.

I saw sculptors and philosophers here, composers and inventors. There were universities, libraries, and laboratories that surpass the wildest inventions of science fiction.

Of the final world I had only a glimpse. Now we no longer seemed to be on earth, but immensely far away, out of all relation to it. And there, still at a great distance, I saw a city—but a city, if such a thing is conceivable, constructed of light. At that time I had not read the Book of Revelation, nor, incidentally, anything on the subject of life after death. But here was a city in which the walls, houses, streets, seemed to give off light, while moving among them were beings as blindingly bright as the One who stood beside me. This was only a moment's vision, for the next instant the walls of the little room closed around me, the dazzling light faded, and a strange sleep stole over me. . . .

I woke up in the hospital bed in that little room, in the familiar world where I'd spent all my life. It was not a homecoming. The cry in my heart that moment has been the cry of my life ever since: Christ, show me Yourself again.

It was weeks before I was well enough to leave the hospital and all that time one thought obsessed me: to get a look at my chart. At last the room was left unattended: there it was in terse medical shorthand, "Pvt. George Ritchie, died December 20, 1943, double lobar pneumonia."

Later, I talked to the doctor who had signed the report. He told me there was no doubt in his mind that I had been dead when he examined me, but that nine minutes later the soldier who had been assigned to prepare me for the morgue had come running to him to ask him to give me a shot of adrenalin. The doctor gave me a hypo of adrenalin directly into the heart muscle, all the while disbelieving what his own eyes were seeing. My return to life, he told me, without brain damage or other lasting effect, was the most baffling circumstance of his career.

Today, over 19 years later, I feel that I know why I had the chance to return to this life. It was to become a physician so that I could learn about man and then serve God. And every time I have been able to serve our God by helping some injured child or counseling some teenager, then deep within I have felt that He was there beside me again.

Fire!

CATHERINE MARSHALL

ON THE evening of December 7, 1946, a businessman, Stuart Luhan (he prefers that his real name not be used), checked into the Winecoff Hotel in Atlanta, Georgia. He asked for and got a room on the tenth floor above the city's traffic.

Sometime after retiring, Mr. Luhan was wakened by noise in the corridor. A strange red glow was reflected in the sky outside his window. *Fire!* Heart pounding, he opened his bedroom door into the corridor only to have billowing clouds of suffocating smoke all but engulf him. Backing into the room, he hastily shut the door and the transom and rushed to the window to fill his lungs with air.

What he saw there was even more terrifying. Ten stories below a crowd was gathering, milling around fire trucks. Behind him, he could hear screams and cries for help.

Fear so consumed him that it was like a weight on his chest. But years before he had formed the habit of setting aside a time each morning for prayer and practice in listening to the Voice inside. From long experience, he knew that he could rely on God in any emergency, even in a burning building.

He retreated to the center of the room and forced himself to begin speaking slowly the Ninety-first Psalm: "Because thou hast made the Lord, which is my refuge, even the most High, thy habitation, there shall no evil befall thee. . . ."

No evil befall thee? In this situation? How could he claim that for himself?

As he repeated this verse, suddenly his thoughts cleared. God is my very life, he reasoned. Therefore that life is eternal. "I hereby put myself in Your care and keeping," he prayed. "Let Your presence be my fortress. I await Your instructions as to the way out of this crisis."

"The first sure sign that God was with me in that fire-surrounded room was that after this prayer my fear just left me, siphoned off like poison," Mr. Luhan wrote me later. "Judging from the sounds around me and the increasing heat in the room, the situation was getting worse by the minute. Yet on the inside was a center of calm, such calmness that I really could hear that inner Voice."

The first instruction was that he should pull on his clothes. The next clear suggestion was to make a rope of the sheets, all blankets, even the bedspread. As he tied the knots, he knew that the rope would not reach more than a third of the way to the street. But he followed instructions, sure he would be told what to do next.

As he put the rope out the window, he heard the Voice say, "No—not yet, trust Me—"

It seemed as if the delay might be fatal. Again the man started to throw the rope out the window. Again the clear order came, "Not yet. . . . Wait."

It took will power to obey, because now black smoke was seeping into the room. But long ago he had learned to trust the Voice of God; it had led him out of other predicaments. Finally the Voice said, "Now is the time. Put the rope out the window. Tie it around the center part of the window frame and climb out."

As Mr. Luhan climbed over the sill, the wood was getting hot. In his mind rang the words, "God is my life and my salvation. . . . I shall not fear. . . . God is my life—"

Across the face of the building he saw a fireman extending a ladder to the eighth floor. That was as far as the ladder would reach. Even so it was still too far away, one room to the right.

Suddenly the fireman saw Mr. Luhan hanging there. He signaled him and swung a rope hanging from a window above toward him. The first time the rope came close; the next time not so close. How could he grasp the swinging rope and still cling to the knotted bedclothes? Once again the rope hurtled through the air. This time Mr. Luhan caught it.

He took a deep breath, twisted the rope around his right hand, let go the knotted bedclothes, and swung in a wide arc across the burning wall. The fireman at the top of the ladder leaned over as far as he dared, caught the end of the rope on which the man dangled, pulled it over. For a moment both men balanced precariously on the slender ladder. Then Stuart Luhan climbed down to safety.

He looked up. His improvised rope was already burning. Flames billowed from the window of the room he had just left. Yet here he was, safe on the ground with no injuries except some rope burns on the palms of his hands. God's timing had been perfect.

We Thought We Heard The Angels Sing

LIEUTENANT JAMES C. WHITTAKER

OUR BIG Liberator bomber rocked gently in the brilliant October sunlight, high above the South Pacific. Looking down through rifts in the drifting clouds we could see the ocean far below, spread out like a vast blue floor. From 5,000 feet it appeared cool and inviting, and I remember thinking it a beautiful sight.

That was on October 18, 1942. Now, three months later, I wonder how I ever could have seen anything of beauty in that shark-ridden waste of mountainous swells and scalding heat. It took the life of one of my companions and clutched at the rest of us, who were saved only by the intervention of God and two divine miracles.

The nose of our ship was pointed toward Hawaii, San Francisco, and home. Tailward lay one of the greatest theaters of war the world has known.

We had picked up our bomber out there and were assigned to set her down on Hickam Field, Honolulu. After that we were to return to the mainland with another ship. This meant brief leaves from duty for all of us and visits home for me.

There were five of us, all members of the United States Army Air Corps, Transport Command. In rank we ranged from Capt. William T. Cherry, Jr., our pilot and commander, to Private John Bartek, our engineer, who also was the youngest. I was within a month of my 41st birthday and was the oldest man on the plane.

The beautiful island of Oahu was rolling up over the rim of sea, and we were nearing the end of the first leg of our trip toward home. As we headed down, the hangars of Hickman Field emerged out of the landscape.

We spent the night of the 19th at the field and whiled away the next day. Shortly after 5 P.M. we collected our gear and started out toward the hangars where our Fortress stood on the line with its four motors warming up.

As we reached the plane our supplies were going aboard; sandwiches, oranges, thermos jugs of coffee. We were about to follow when we were hailed and learned shortly that our plans had been changed.

We had been reassigned to carry the world-famous Capt. Eddie Rickenbacker and a military aide upon a secret mission for the War Department. We were keenly disappointed. But an order is an order.

We fired up our engines at 1:29 A.M. of October 21 and one minute later were shooting down the runway. I adjusted the DF (direction finding) set to the Honolulu tower's frequency for takeoff instructions. The big ship lifted easily, and we were in the air. We climbed straight away from the field through a haze and cloud ceiling into clear air.

Our immediate destination was Island X, about 1,700 miles southwest of the Hawaiian group. We droned along at from 8,000 to 10,000 feet, high above the cloud bank.

Bill Cherry had been turning up the radio and tinkering with the DF control to get a bearing on the radio compass.

"Jim," he asked, looking puzzled, "did this thing work okay during the takeoff this morning?"

"Sure," I told him. "What's the matter?"

"It won't budge an inch now."

It should be explained that in order to locate stations, there is a directional loop, up outside the fuselage. This is turned by means of a crank which extends downward into the cockpit. I tried turning it and found it would move only a few degrees of the circle it was supposed to describe.

I continued to try while Cherry took the controls and started nosing us down from our 10,000 foot altitude. We were nearing our ETA (estimated time of arrival). The crank still refused to turn.

This became a minor matter, however, when DeAngelis came up, looking worried. Our ETA actually had passed. We were down below the overcast and there was no island in sight.

We had missed the island, passing either northeast or southwest of it. Then we remembered the octant which had smashed against the side of the plane during the groundloop. Undoubtedly it had been thrown out of adjustment and consequently had showed us as being dead on course while actually we had been veering away.

There was nothing to do but face it, and Bill Cherry put it into words in his forthright Texas fashion.

"We're lost," he said—just like that.

I saw Cherry's face grow glum. He told Rickenbacker:

"That tears it. The station is about 1,000 miles away."

"How much fuel have you?" Rick asked.

'Enough for about four hours," Bill replied. This was enough to get us only a little more than three quarters of the distance we would have to go.

"What do you expect to do now?" Rickenbacker asked.

"We'll try the box procedure first," Cherry replied.

Cherry figured that if we should fly 45 minutes on each leg of the box, we still would have about an hour's fuel when we finished.

I searched the far rims of the cloudbank, the blue vaults of sky above us, and the watery blue floor far below. Never have I seen a world so ominously empty.

As the last of our three hours ticked off, Bill summoned Reynolds.

"Go on emergency frequency and start pounding our S O S," he said. "Someone will hear us and get a bearing on our course."

"Jim," he continued, "we will have to set her down in about an hour. Let's talk about how we are going to do it."

So far as either of us knew then, no four-motored land plane ever had been set down at sea without casualties. In many cases no member of the crew had lived to tell about it.

When a plane is put into the ocean against the wind, it meets the waves head on. If it touches on a crest, the nose will be plunged into the next wave and cave in. Further, the ship probably will not float an instant, but will continue its dive through the water.

If the plane hits the first crest too hard, it breaks in two and the parts disappear almost immediately. It is inevitable that the crew will be stunned for a few instants by a crash landing and in such a case Davy Jones has ample time to snatch them down.

I suggested, therefore, that we come in cross wind and set the ship down in a trough—the valley between two waves. Bill added:

"I think we ought to do it while we've still got gasoline in the tanks. A power landing is always better than an uncontrolled one."

Rick led everyone except Reynolds to the compartment aft of the bomb bay and had them lie down, their heads toward the tail and their feet braced against the bulkhead.

We didn't know how much fuel was left and, needing it all,

we cut the two inboard motors at about 500 feet and feathered the propellers to prevent them turning in the wind. Rick had got the aft deck trap open and was dropping equipment and luggage out to lighten the plane.

We heard the voice of DeAngelis who had come up behind us.

"Do you fellows mind," he asked, "if I pray?"

"What do you think we're doing?" Bill Cherry snapped without lifting his eyes. DeAngelis returned to the others and in a moment Rickenbacker's voice sang out, clear and calm:

"Fifty feet!" and almost immediately: "Thirty feet!"

"Twenty feet!"

It was strangely still in the plane. The muffled roar of the two outboard engines seemed far away. There was a faint whooshing of wind against the fuselage. The whine of Reynolds's radio rose above it, sharp and insistent.

"Ten feet!"

The wind was a roar now, howling into the open traps. We were coming in at 90 miles an hour with the landing flaps and wheels up so there would be nothing to snag in the water.

"Five feet!" Rickenbacker shouted. "Three feet! . . . One foot!"

"Cut it!" yelled Bill.

I pulled the mainline switch, killing every electrical connection in the plane. Bill hauled back on the wheel, hooking the tail into the water. The fuselage went down into the trough and lunged, but did not leave the surface. The waves rolled up about us. We were in. From 90 miles an hour we came to a full stop in a little over 30 feet—about 10 steps.

The shock and pressure of that landing is almost indescribable to a person who has never been through one. Despite the cushions, the safety belt seemed to be slicing me in two. A taste of bitter vinegar filled my mouth.

My eyes seemed to spin around like already taut springs

winding up to the snapping point. I couldn't see. I thought I was losing consciousness.

A final slash of the safety belt and the pressure inside my head reduced swiftly. My bursting eyes began to unwind. I don't remember leaving my seat, but the next I knew I was up, yanking the rip cord that freed the forward one of two five-place rubber rafts above the fuselage. Rickenbacker was freeing the aft raft. DeAngelis and Kaczmarczyk were shoving the tiny, three man raft up through the escape hatch over the bomb bay.

Bill Cherry was scrambling out of the pilot's seat unscathed. Blood was streaming from a cut across Reynolds's nose. I heard Col. Adamson calling out as though in great pain that his shoulder had been wrenched. I had a slight arm cut.

I don't know the order in which we left the ship. For the first time in history a four-motored land plane had been put down into the ocean without serious casualties. And I wanted to keep it that way. We got out fast.

When we were clear of the plane, we unshipped our aluminum oars. Rick had some line, which we used to fasten the rafts together.

The only food was four anemic oranges which we found floating in the water. We handed these over to Col. Adamson after deciding on a ration of one-eighth of an orange a day per man.

A swift movement beside our raft caught my eye and I turned for a better look. I saw something that had so far escaped the notice of us all, and the shock I got was almost as severe as the one during our crash landing.

The water about the raft fleet was alive with the triangular, dorsal fins of sharks.

Our raft plunged into a deep trough. When we came up I was busy for a minute with our line. When I looked up again, our plane was gone. I am glad I didn't see her go.

In a few minutes the sun had disappeared. It was as if an

electric light had been snapped off, so quickly did the equatorial dusk descend. The three quarter moon appeared, and we could see from one raft to another quite easily.

Dawn of the second day broke clear. We stretched as best we could in our cramped positions to work off our grogginess. We soon found that, in addition, we were working up terrific appetites. And there was no food.

As the sun rose higher, Rick gave some good advice to us all. The first thing was to protect our heads from the direct rays. This we did with undergarments—those of us who had no hats or caps. Rick advised us to move around as little as possible, thus conserving energy. We talked as little as possible to avoid drying our mouths.

It was time for breakfast. Col. Adamson took out one of the four little oranges and peeled it. Each man got a segment. Except for the pleasant taste, we might as well have not had anything.

The value of Rick's advice became obvious about 11 A.M. when the sun neared the zenith. We were in equatorial waters, and the rays beat almost straight down. They felt like molten metal.

When the terrible heat had passed, we sat about in a sort of daze. So great was the relief that we almost forgot our hunger. Our craving for water, however, was becoming more and more insistent.

As I sat there that evening in our second day adrift, I noticed that Johnny Bartek was reading his Testament. It was cold.

We welcomed the rising sun of October 23—our third day afloat—even though we knew it soon would be roasting us alive.

We were red and were sunburning despite our efforts to protect our skins. The reflected glare from the water was partially responsible. Windburn had a share in it too. And the salt deposited by the spray was beginning to sting us.

The fourth day found our hunger agonizing. The fish hooks

Johnny DeAngelis had brought along were useless because we had no bait. The fish could not be tempted with the bare hooks.

When we had stretched ourselves, Col. Adamson produced our next to last orange. We got no physical benefit from our tiny segments, but they moistened the mouth, and we had come to look forward to the daily dole.

As I considered that tomorrow we would have our last one, I began to weigh the possibility that our situation might be desperate. We had seen no sign of ship or plane.

There was a loud flapping of wings. Without warning and as natural as anything, a sea swallow alighted on Rickenbacker's head.

We held our breath.

The bird looked curiously at each of us in turn. Rick's hand moved up slowly. He rubbed his chin. He caressed his nose. He smoothed an eyebrow. Then, with a swift snatch, he made the bird prisoner.

Rick carved him up. I got a leg. And let me say here and now that I will have to be starving before I ever taste sea swallow again. Not only is the flesh rank, but the muscles are like iron wires. I will say, however, sea swallow plumbing makes excellent bait.

We pulled the rafts together and handed our catch over to the Colonel. He carved with one of the sheath knives. Each of us received a fish steak about an inch square and just a little over half an inch thick.

Everyone felt pretty blue. At length Bartek got out his Testament, and we pulled the rafts together for a prayer meeting. We said the Lord's prayer. I should make it clear that the others said the Lord's prayer. I only knew a word here and there.

I was exposed to religion and Bible in my boyhood, but lost it all in the years after. My feeling that day on the raft was a considerable modification of my impatience when DeAngelis had asked to pray as the plane was heading down into the sea.

Col. Adamson read from the 31st through the 34th verses of the sixth chapter of Matthew:

" 'Therefore, take ye no thought, saying: What shall we eat? or What shall we drink? or, Wherewithal shall we be clothed? For these are things the heathen seeketh. For your Heavenly Father knoweth that you have need of all these things. But seek ye first the kingdom of God, and His righteousness; and all these things shall be added unto you. Take therefore no thought for the morrow; for the morrow shall take thought for the things of itself. Sufficient unto the day is the evil thereof.' "

As the coppery sun shot into the sky on our sixth day adrift, we all began to realize the gravity of our situation. It had been almost 120 hours since our Flying Fortress had disappeared beneath the waves.

During that time each of us had had three minnows, one morsel of raw fish, and a fragment of sea swallow in the way of solid food. We also had moistened our mouths with three segments of orange. We had drunk no water since we left the plane.

When the cool of evening finally came, it was quite a while before we could summon the energy to assemble the rafts and open our prayer service. As Col. Adamson began to read from Bartek's Testament, it appeared ridiculous to me that men as practical as we and as hardboiled could expect a mumbling voice out on that waste of water to summon help for us.

However, I joined passively in the prayers. I found I was learning the Lord's prayer. I could start with the rest and finish the first two lines. And, of course, I could join in on the "Amen." There was a general prayer for food in which I joined, still passively.

Cherry finished his verse from Matthew. His voice went on. I realized with a start that Cherry was praying. He was addressing the Lord as "Old Master." He was saying it with deference and reverence; simply and directly.

"Old Master, we know this isn't a guarantee we'll eat in the morning. But we're in an awful fix, as You know. We sure are counting on a little something by day after tomorrow, at least. See what You can do for us, Old Master."

Cherry finished his talk to God. Then he fired off our evening flare in the hope that something might happen. And it did!

The flare's propulsion charge was faulty, and the flaming ball rose 50 feet or so into the air, then fell back among the rafts. It hissed and zigzagged around the water. The dazzling red light illuminated the ocean for hundreds of yards, and in the depths we could see barracuda playing havoc with a school of fish attracted by the glare.

Two fair-sized specimens, pursued by the barracuda, broke water and plumped into our raft. We had just time to grab them when the flare sputtered and died. The moon came out and shed a ghostly light on the ocean. Fish were for breakfast, but I was too puzzled to sleep.

When the sun's rays were almost horizontal and our shadows stretched far out across the water to the eastward, we assembled for prayer. As happens when you are starving, our desire for food had gradually diminished. But the terrible cravings of a man dying of thirst never diminish. His last moments before lapsing into coma are his most agonizing.

So it was that on this night we prayed for water rather than for food. Except in the verses from Matthew, I don't think food was mentioned.

When the group prayer had been completed, Cherry addressed the Lord in his forthright fashion:

"Old Master, we called on You for food and You delivered. We ask You now for water. We've done the best we could. If you don't make up Your mind to help us pretty soon, I guess that's all there'll be to it. It looks like the next move is up to You, Old Master."

While we rolled and wallowed over the crests and into the troughs, I was thinking that this was God's chance to make a believer of Jim Whittaker. If there was indeed a God and He could ignore a prayer like that, then He must be a pretty heartless being.

My thoughts went on in this vein for some time; I don't know how long. I do know that eventually I became aware something was tugging insistently at my consciousness. I looked over to the left. A cloud that had been fleecy and white a while ago now was darkening by the second.

While I watched a bluish curtain unrolled from the cloud to sea. It was rain—and moving toward us! Now everyone saw the downpour, sweeping across the ocean and speckling the waves with giant drops.

"Here she is!" Cherry shouted. "Thanks, Old Master!" Another minute and we were being deluged by sheets of cold water that splashed into our parched mouths and sluiced the caked salt off our burned and stinging bodies. We cupped our hands to guide the life-giving rivulets down our throats.

For a time we could think only of the blessed relief of the moment. Then the more practical minds began turning toward the days ahead which might hold as much privation as had those just ended. We looked about for storage facilities.

The only reservoirs immediately available were our Mae Wests. As the valve openings into them were very small, we hit upon this plan: We soaked and wrung out our shirts until all the salt was washed out of them. Then we saturated them again and wrung the water into our mouths. It was easy in this way to deposit it into the life jackets, closing the valve afterward. The rain lashed down nearly an hour, soothing our bodies and quenching our thirst.

At prayers after our scalding ninth day, I joined feelingly in the worship. I wanted to believe.

The rising sun of our tenth day disclosed that all the men except me had fallen victims to the scourge deep-water men dread—salt water ulcers.

Cherry handed out the last of the water that morning. We doubled and twisted the life jacket to get the last drop out of it and looked longingly at the dampness.

The waterless afternoon in the equatorial heat seemed to take something out of us, physically and mentally. That evening Bill Cherry led the Lord's prayer, which I knew pretty well by now. Then each fellow prayed individually.

I could tell more about those prayers; the promises made to God to lead new lives if He should spare them. But it wouldn't be right to identify the men with their supplications.

On the tenth evening, Bill Cherry again spoke to the Lord, in behalf of us all, addressing him as usual as "Old Master." After acknowledging that Providence had saved us more than once, Cherry put it this way:

"You wouldn't have let us live this long if You didn't intend to save us after a while, would You, Old Master? We need some more of that rain, and we need it in the worst way. How's about it, Old Master?"

Throughout the late watches of the chilling night, I sat sleeplessly thinking over our condition and the state of my own soul. It was not a pleasant line of thought.

I had been an agnostic; an atheist, if you will. I imagined that I doubted the existence of such a being as God. I reasoned further, when religion was mentioned, that God never had done much for me in my life, so why should I go through the motions of worshiping Him?

I pondered that night on an expression I had heard somewhere out in the Southwest Pacific: "There are no atheists in the foxholes of Guadalcanal." I can tell you now that there can be no atheists in rubber rafts amid whitecaps and sharks in the equatorial Pacific.

I was finding my God in those watery wastes, and we were meeting as strangers. We might have remained strangers had it not been for Him. He soon was to send the two divine miracles that twice more were to save my life and change the way of it about as completely as a life can be changed.

The 13th day adrift burst upon us as a scorcher. Just after 10 o'clock a rain squall blotted out the sun. Our hopes rose. The familiar blue curtain of rain moved toward us across the sea. We prayed aloud for it to reach us. It was less than a quarter of a mile off when a perverse wind shunted it away.

Somehow, my faith did not die. For the first time I found myself leading the rest in prayer.

"God," I prayed, "You know what that water means to us. The wind has blown it away. It is in Your power, God, to send back that rain. It's nothing to You, but it means life to us."

"God, the wind is Yours. You own it. Order it to blow back that rain to us who will die without it."

There are some things that can't be explained by natural law. The wind did not change, but the receding curtain of rain stopped where it was. Then, ever so slowly, it started back toward us—against the wind! It was as if a great and omnipotent hand was guiding it to us across the water.

We caught a great store of water and luxuriated as the cool deluge flooded down our bodies. Many of the men had shed skin three or four times by now. There were raw spots where they had chafed against the walls of the narrow rafts. In addition, the ulcers were growing worse hourly.

Those men will know until the end of their days what it means to have salt in a wound. The cool rain that came from the skies was their only relief.

The rain that came that day was a Godsend. Without this relief I don't know how we would have got through the four days of doldrums that were just ahead and which were to be the most terrible part of our ordeal.

In our days of drifting along the equator we had had our share of the rains and sudden squalls that mark that section of the Pacific. And on the morning of the 14th day we went into the doldrums. There was no breeze at dawn nor did any arise during the day.

It was to be the worst period of the entire three weeks for more reasons than thirst and hunger. About me was suffering such as I never had seen before. Of the seven survivors I was the only one whose lower body was not a mass of ulcers.

And now our clothing was disintegrating. The violent sun rays were beginning to inflict serious burns. My socks had gone to pieces and my shirt was splitting down the back, the sleeves, and the front. I had left my shoes on the plane.

We had water, but the tiny daily dole in the bottom of the flare shell only made us thirstier. Hunger had so weakened us that the slightest effort was exhausting. We hadn't eaten in days, because the salt air had rotted the fish lines, enabling the sharks to snap them and carry off the hooks. Anyway, we had no bait.

Dawn of our 18th day found me in the stern of our raft brooding in a half wakeful stupor. Our morale, I was thinking, had sunk just about as low as it could go. Nothing could depress us farther. And, as usual, I was wrong.

During that day, the day after, and the 20th day we were dealt such crushing blows that had it not been for the fortitude built up in hours of prayer I think we all would have abandoned hope.

At the prayer service I reminded God of the miracle of the rain on the 13th day. I prayed as never before for rescue; not just for water or food, but to be picked up. Memory of the rain miracle seemed to bear me up. As the service closed, I felt that rescue was coming. I prayed again that I might live to see it.

We had had our evening dole of water and were sitting silent. I happened to be looking at Bill Cherry. Suddenly he sat up. There was a sort of wild look in his eyes.

"I hear an engine!" he yelled. "I hear an engine! Hear it?"

We ALL had heard it; a deep toned roar, muted by distance. Rickenbacker and Cherry saw it at the same time; a plane silhouetted against a low cloud bank in the west and coming in our general direction.

The plane was coming fast, and we soon could see that its course would take it past us at least three miles distant.

I now reviewed mentally the things that God had done for me since that day so long ago when our gallant Flying Fortress disappeared beneath the waves. I thought of the answers I had received to prayer. But most of all I thought of the more important thing—that I had learned to pray. And that I had found my God and had not turned away from Him a stranger.

Our sufferings were not ended, and I didn't try to kid myself that they were. I was weaker from hunger than I ever had been in my life. I was so thirsty my throat ached. Yet within me there was a lift that made these other things seem trivial. I prayed—a prayer of thanksgiving.

Shortly after dawn of the 19th day the scout plane came over again. It was flying at about 1,200 feet, and it missed us by three miles. The ship came back in the afternoon at the same height, but we were closer to its course this time.

Each time it appeared we almost went out of our heads with excitement. Its pilot still failed to see us.

On the 20th morning, while we were waiting for the early patrol plane to pass over—and not see us—Bill Cherry spoke abruptly:

"Listen, you fellows," he said, "I think it's time we were giving Providence a little help. I'm taking the small raft and cutting loose by myself. If we all spread over a wider area we'll have a 3 to 1 better chance of being seen. When one raft is found, they'll start a real search and pick up the others."

There was little sleep in our raft that night. We were lonesome for the following in the other boats, for one thing. But there was something else. My feeling of the night before that something big was just ahead kept me wakeful.

In the last hour before light I fell into a deep sleep—and slept through the most important dawn of the three weeks. I had strained my eyes in 20 dawns only to have the rising light disclose an empty ocean, an empty sky, an empty world.

I opened my eyes to our 21st day adrift to find DeAngelis shaking me as roughly as his failing strength would permit. He was gripping my shoulder and calling my name.

"Jim" he said, "I think you'd better take a look. It may be a mirage, but I think I see something."

I rolled over in the raft and sat up. There was no need for him to point. And it was no mirage. Across the horizon stretched a line of palm trees about 10 miles long. At that distance, about 12 miles, I couldn't see any actual land. But I felt safe in assuming there would be something substantial under those palms.

At 6:30 A.M. of Nov. 11, I broke out our two aluminum oars and began what was to be a 7½ hour pull to put dry land under our feet. My two raft mates were in pitiable condition. DeAngelis could still move about, and that was all.

Jimmy Reynolds lay prone in the raft. He was preciously near the finish. His eyes had sunk an inch and a half into his skull. His resemblance to a death's head was startling. Jimmy's normal weight is 130 pounds. He weighed 90 a few days later when Navy Doctors got to him.

During that long row to the island Jimmy lay against the gunwale behind me and with the flare shell dipped water which he poured on the back of my head and neck after the heat began to bear down after 10 o'clock. Without it I might have collapsed.

We had calculated to get in about noon, and I was encouraged by the good time I made. Just before 12 o'clock we had reached a point less than 250 yards from the shore. Then something happened.

The boat careened and went out of control. Another second or two and we were racing back out to sea. Nothing I could do with the oars was any help. The wild current held us until we were far out; a mile or so, at least.

The long narrow island was moving slowly across our bow like a giant ocean liner, crawling out to sea. We were drifting, though it seemed the island was leaving us, instead. We had started for the head of the island and now were more than half way down it.

If ever I have cried out in anguish, it was then. I was done, finished, washed up. I called Heaven to witness that I was whipped. I could hardly hold on to the light oars. Yet there within reach was the land—and life. And while I watched, that line of majestic palms continued to move away, with terrible deliberation. If we were to reach land at all, it would have to be now.

I tried to move my numbed fingers and aching arms. It was no use. Only a miracle could set our feet on that island, I thought; only a miracle. A miracle! I remembered the miracle of the rain on the 13th day. I remembered other answers to prayer. I remembered my God!

I cried out to Him to give me strength. I shouted it above the rising wind in the fear He might not hear. I caught a glimpse of DeAngelis's startled face. Still shouting, I lifted the oars. I rowed.

Half an hour later I was still rowing—and making progress. When the treacherous current had shot us out to sea, I had been powerless to hold the boat against it. Now I was overcoming that current.

I was overcoming it in the face of obstacles and hazards that hadn't beset me before. I have spoken of the rising wind. It brought a deluge of rain that all but blotted out the island. I turned about in the raft and adopted the fisherman's stroke that I might see ahead and better direct our course.

An oar jerked and turned in my hand. I glanced that way in

time to see a dirty gray form, 12 feet long, disappearing beneath the waves. As I watched, another shark surfaced, slashed at the oar, and slid under. These sharks were not the droll dullards that had plagued us earlier. These were man eaters. If they should attack the raft, we were gone.

The rain slackened and I could see the island, still moving away in the mist. I cried out my final prayer:

"God! Don't quit me now!"

I have described the miracle of the rain. I have told of the flare that went faulty and became the means of providing fish for us to eat after our desperate prayer for food.

The prayer I uttered that afternoon was more than desperate. It was an anguished supplication shouted above the wind and the rain. It came from the depths of my soul. And there were no mental reservations this time. I was calling to my God, who alone could save us. The answer was immediate and miraculous; it was the second of the two divine miracles.

Strength surged back into my shoulders and arms. I slashed at the man-eating sharks with the oars. They wheeled as though about to attack. But I didn't care. I was rowing again. I was rowing and bending those aluminum oars against the white caps. I say it was I who was bending them. That isn't true. Of himself, Jim Whittaker couldn't have bent a pin.

As the raft rolled steadily through the foam, I was not conscious of exerting any strength. Indeed, it was as though the oars were working automatically and my hands merely following their motions. There were other hands than mine on those oars.

I am considered a good boatman, and I am naturally strong. Yet today, fully recovered in strength, I would hesitate to tackle that stretch of water. Then, I was thoroughly exhausted, and there were three weeks of thirst, hunger, and suffering behind me.

The rain was coming down in torrents. The sharks had doubled in number and appeared to be massing for the attack, whizzing past us and slashing at the oars.

Yet as steadily as though drawn by a cable attached to a steam winch on shore, we moved through the treacherous surface, amid the sharks, and in the face of a buffeting rain squall. It was the second miracle, and I recognized it for what it was.

As we neared the foam that marked the reef, we faced a new danger. The ebb was not quite over yet, and with the rollers coming in the sharp coral might easily puncture the raft air chambers.

Johnny DeAngelis lay across the bow, pulling and guiding with his hands. Using the lift given us by the swells, we inched the vulnerable rubber boat across the reef and into the calmer water beyond.

The miraculous strength that had come to me out there in the storm sustained me until our bow grounded soundlessly. It was our first solid land in three weeks. The time was 2 P.M. on Nov. 11th, 1942.

These are the things I told daily for weeks before armies of airplane workers, steel workers, and ship builders. And I told them the story of the rafts; how during those blazing days out there I found my God. I will tell that story again and again, so long as I live. It was the greatest adventure a man can have. It is the greatest story a man can tell.